Hard Sayings

Hard Sayings

Understanding Difficult Passages of Scripture

R.C. SPROUL

 LIGONIER MINISTRIES

Hard Sayings: Understanding Difficult Passages of Scripture
© 2023 by the R.C. Sproul Trust

Published by Ligonier Ministries
421 Ligonier Court, Sanford, FL 32771
Ligonier.org

Printed in China
Amity Printing Company
0001223
First edition, second printing

ISBN 978-1-64289-461-5 (Hardcover)
ISBN 978-1-64289-462-2 (ePub)

Cover design: Ligonier Creative
Interior design and typeset: Katherine Lloyd, The DESK

Ligonier Ministries edited and adapted Dr. R.C. Sproul's original material to create this volume. We are thankful to Mrs. Vesta Sproul for her invaluable help on this project.

Scripture quotations are from the ESV® Bible (The Holy Bible, English Standard Version®), copyright © 2001 by Crossway, a publishing ministry of Good News Publishers. Used by permission. All rights reserved.

Library of Congress Control Number: 2022938425

Contents

Introduction

The concept of *hard sayings* in Scripture is often talked about. But what does it mean? What makes a saying hard? It turns out that there are different ways that a saying can appear hard to us. In fact, the hard sayings of Scripture can be broken into three different categories.

In the first place, a saying of Scripture may be a hard saying if it appears to us to be somewhat harsh in its orientation. In that sense, it's hard to swallow because these statements can jar or jolt us and harm our sensibilities, and we recoil from them. We read, for example, in the Old Testament that God instructed the Israelites to institute the *herem*, which had to do with the wholesale destruction of the Canaanite nation—man, woman, and child—and that seems so harsh and severe. It seems to cast a shadow on the love of God, on the mercy of God, and on the goodness of God. We say "How do we handle texts like that? They're difficult, they're hard" because they are severe to our senses. That's one category of hard saying.

The second category of hard sayings is one that's hard to understand. That is, our interpretation of its meaning is somewhat enigmatic and problematic. Such sayings are hard to understand, not because of their harshness but because they are difficult for us to unravel. For example, much of what the Bible teaches is about the sovereignty of God and His sovereign control over human behavior, coupled with the responsibility that we have as volitional agents and being responsible for the choices that we make. How do we put those things together? That's difficult, and so we can call those sayings *hard sayings*.

The third category, similar to the second, is a hard saying that has become controversial in the history of biblical interpretation, usually because of one of the first two reasons.

In this book, we will explore some of the more prominent hard sayings of Scripture. But let me say one thing by way of preface, as a way of commending to you the study of hard sayings. If there is a shortcut to accelerating your understanding of Scripture, it is to focus your attention on such passages. When you read through the Bible and you come upon a text that bothers you, you don't have to be paralyzed and stop there and stay there forever. Move on, but mark it; if you find a passage you don't understand, put a red mark next to it, and then later on, come back and focus on those red marks. Say: "Here's a portion of Scripture that I don't understand. I'm going to devote special attention to trying to understand these passages that are difficult." That is a great way to learn. If you focus on the obstacles to your progress and remove them one by one, you'll have an augmented understanding.

Even more important are those texts that jar your emotions, and when you read them you say, "I don't like what the Bible says here." Put a big mark next to those passages in Scripture that offend you, that at first glance you disagree with. Those are the ones that you need to put your focus on if you want to grow rapidly. If you do so, one of two things will happen. You may discover that the reason that that text offended you or annoyed your sensitivities was that you didn't understand it. After you delve into it and examine it, read resources about it, and come to a better insight of what it means, your problem may be resolved, you can move on, and in the meantime, you've gained new insight and new understanding.

But suppose that you check all the resources, you're careful in your examination of the text, you find out that you understand it exactly right, and it still makes you mad and you don't like it. For example, you may read, "Wives, submit to your husbands" (Col. 3:18). "I don't like that," you say. Put three checks next to that passage because your reaction means one of two things. Either there's something wrong with the author of Scripture who wrote those words—in this case, there would be something wrong with Paul's thinking and Paul ought to change—or there's something wrong with your thinking because here, while you're being critical of Scripture, Scripture is being critical of you.

If you want to grow in grace and in sanctification, find those places where you are critical of God. It might just be that these are the places where you need to change your thinking and your life.

1

Without Form
and Void

Genesis 1

A s we consider the hard sayings of the Bible, we're going to begin with the Old Testament. In fact, we're going to start on page 1 with the very first chapter of Genesis and look at a controversial text that appears as early as the second verse of sacred Scripture.

Let's look, then, at Genesis 1:2. To set it in context, we need to read verse 1 before we read verse 2. Genesis begins with these words: "In the beginning, God created the heavens and the earth." That is verse 1. The hard saying, or the controversial verse, follows immediately in verse 2: "The earth was without form and void, and darkness was over the face of the deep." Now, that's just the first part of verse 2. Here is the rest of the verse: "And the Spirit of God was hovering over the face of the waters." It is this first segment of Genesis 1:2 that is our hard saying; it's hard because of the controversy that attends the interpretation of it.

Actually, two different controversies have been attached to the understanding of Genesis 1:2. The first has to do with the third word of the verse. In the English Standard Version, it reads, "The earth was without form." In the early *Scofield Reference Bible*, however, the notation there indicates that the verse should be translated this way: "And the earth *became* without form and void." You can immediately see the difference in meaning between those variant interpretations. It's one thing to say that the earth *was* without form and void and quite another to say that the earth *became* without form and void, because the presumption is that if it became without form and void, there must have been something else before it in order for it to become something.

Around this interpretation, the old *Scofield Reference Bible* constructed a theory of biblical interpretation that conditioned the whole scope of understanding the entire book of Genesis. That theory is known by one of two names. The common view is what is called the *gap theory*; the more technical term for it is the *restoration hypothesis*. The restoration hypothesis is just that—it's a hypothesis. It's a speculative attempt to explain some significant problems in reconciling the biblical account of creation with certain modern theories of the emergence of the universe out of primordial materials. It's called the gap theory because it suggests that only one verse in the book of Genesis refers to God's initial work of creation, and that is verse 1. Now, of course, the book of Genesis does not have a title in the original manuscript. It's not called Genesis; that's the title that has been added throughout history by the Jews and then subsequently by the Christians in establishing the names of the books of the canon. We are accustomed to thinking that the book of Genesis is called by that name because the book is concerned with teaching something about the beginning of the universe—the genesis of the universe in which we live. If we were to follow the gap theory, we would say that only one verse in the book of Genesis refers to the original work of divine creation—namely, Genesis 1:1. Then what follows, beginning in verse 2, is an account not of the original creation of the universe but of the re-creation or regeneration of a creation that had fallen into a state of chaos. So then, it would perhaps be better to title the book of Genesis the book of Re-Genesis. The idea is that there is a historical gap between verse 1 and verse 2. The gap, which could be as long as several million years or even billions of years, would mean that what we read about the six days of original creation refers instead to the six days of re-creation rather than the original work of God.

Before I look at this further in terms of interpretation, let me say a word about why such a hypothesis emerged in the first place. One of the big reasons that people struggle with the trustworthiness of sacred Scripture has to do with the onslaught of the reliability of the biblical description of creation in light of modern scientific theories, particularly with respect to the age of the earth. There is an ongoing debate today, even within the Christian community, with respect to the antiquity of the earth. Is the earth of recent origin, say six thousand years or so ago, or is the creation of the universe something that, as most modern astronomers and scientists claim, took place fifteen to eighteen billion years ago? That's quite a huge discrepancy, and Christians are engaged in debates often over the age of the earth. Even the evangelical world is divided between old-earthers and young-earthers.

The gap theory conveniently solves the dilemma of the age of the earth by saying that the Bible gives only one verse to the original creation, which could have happened thousands, millions, or billions of years ago, and that what is being described in the rest of Genesis 1 is of much more recent origin—namely, the restoration of a creation that had undergone a cataclysmic, catastrophic fall between verse 1 and verse 2. Allusions in some of the poetic literature later on in the Prophets and in Job refer to the cosmic upheaval in heaven with the fall of Satan. In Genesis 1:1 you have the original creation where everything was good, followed by a gap when this cosmic catastrophe happens with the fall of the angels with Satan, the plunging of the universe into ruin, and finally God's repairing the damage beginning in verse 2. If this is the case, we read about the repairing of that damage in the rest of the opening chapters of Genesis.

From a literary perspective, the whole thing virtually hinges on the interpretation of the verb here in Hebrew. In almost every translation of the Bible, the verb is translated as the English word "was," but according to the gap theory or the restitution hypothesis, it should be translated as "became." The word "was" would indicate the state in which it was in the initial aspect of creation, and as I mentioned earlier, the word "became" would suggest a dramatic change of some sort. The verb used here occurs hundreds of times in the Bible, and in any Hebrew lexicon, the primary meaning of the word is "was." Now, it is true that in less than 1 percent of its occurrences in Hebrew, it can be and is sometimes—though rarely—translated as the English word "became." So the translator does have the option when he comes to a text that uses this word to render it as "was" or as "became." When that happens, the normal method of biblical translation is to use the primary, usual meaning of the term unless there is compelling reason to use the other meaning. Such a compelling reason is usually discovered in the immediate context of the text or in the broader context of biblical usage.

In this case, the preference to use "became" rather than "was" is not so much driven by the immediate context, though it includes that, which I'll address momentarily. It seems that the major motivation here is this contemporary philosophical problem in reconciling the idea of a young earth and a late creation date with the scientific claims that run to the contrary. As good as it is to engage in apologetics, this is not a compelling reason to translate the text this way. Translation must be done according to the demands of the context and not according to other concerns that lead to linguistically or hermeneutically suspect readings.

Proponents of the gap theory do, however, make an appeal to the context to reinforce the translation "became." Again, the gap theory says that the earth "became" without form and "became" void and "became" dark in terms of the deep. Proponents argue from the text that it's somehow beneath the dignity of God to create anything in a state of formlessness, darkness, and emptiness, particularly because these three descriptive terms of the void, the darkness, and the emptiness suggest a picture not of orderliness and harmony but of an ominous, threatening, chaotic creation that is not overcome until the Holy Spirit does His transforming work of hovering over the waters of the deep and bringing substance into the emptiness and light into the darkness and order into the disorder.

In other Near Eastern mythological accounts of creation (such as the Babylonian view), there is a common theme of the universe's coming into being as a result of a cosmic primordial struggle between forces of good and forces of evil, between forces of darkness and forces of light. The principal poetic or mythological image is that of gods struggling with a primordial sea monster that dwells in the abyss of the deep. Along similar lines, we could see the biblical account of creation as telling of a catastrophic fall that plunges the world into chaos, with the old serpent, Satan, ruling over things. Then we hear of the victory of God over the forces of chaos, over the forces of Satan, over the sea monster who inhabits the deep, and so on. That's another reason that some have argued for a gap between Genesis 1:1 and 1:2.

The historic and classical biblical interpretation of Genesis 1:2 is not that it simply describes chaos or some threatening, ominous evil that is part of the original creation but that, as Martin Luther and the Reformers and others throughout history have argued, Genesis 1:2 is simply a description of the not-yet-ordered, incomplete work of divine creation. The thematic statement of verse 1 refers to God's original work of creation, and in the biblical account of that initial creation, before God separates the dark from the light and before He creates any luminaries such as the sun, there would have been a darkness. Before He fills the earth with creeping things, flying things, fish, animals, plants, and everything, there would have been a certain emptiness, and a predominance of water would be consistent with our understanding of how the world is constructed even today. If one looks at planet Earth from a spaceship or sees a photograph taken from outer space, the color of our planet is obviously blue, which reflects the massive amount of water that covers the globe. This historic interpretation does not see Genesis 1:2 as describing some kind of cosmic battle between God and an equal, opposite force of evil or the force of darkness but instead sees it as simply referring to the beginning stages of divine creation, which are then spelled out in greater detail through the rest of the chapter. This is the beginning superstructure for creation, the outline, if you will, as it would be before the details are filled in.

I'm sure the controversy over creation will continue to rage. As it does, it's helpful to understand this particular controversy and why people are exercised over it. Certainly the gap theory is a possible interpretation of Genesis 1:2. But I am persuaded that though it is a literary possibility and even a theological possibility, there really is no compelling reason to assume it.

When we look at problems such as we find in the opening chapters of Genesis, we have to exercise a certain kind of caution and a certain kind of patience. We must realize that in our contemporary culture there is probably no dimension of the Christian truth claims that is more under attack from the secular world than the foundational question of creation. In the history of philosophy, one of the reasons that the Christian church received a high degree of intellectual credibility in the Middle Ages and in the European medieval university system, even from those who did not profess faith in Christianity, was that the secular thinkers of that day found it difficult to avoid the conclusion that something had to create this universe in the first place. So it's not a surprise that the central aim of skepticism against Christianity, even against religion in general, is at the point of creation. If the idea of a creator can be eliminated, then the whole rest of the message of Scripture falls.

2

Created in Six Days, Part 1

Genesis 1–2; Exodus 20

In this chapter, we're going to take up a hard saying that causes great controversy not only between the church and secular thinkers but also among professing Christians. This major point of division is whether the universe was created in six twenty-four-hour days. Are we to believe that the world came into being in six literal days, or is there another option for understanding the time frame of creation? Closely related to this is the question of how recent the origin of the universe and the appearance of human life on this planet is. Initially, we will look at a text not in Genesis but in Exodus, where we will see reference to the Sabbath in the giving of the Ten Commandments. Exodus 20:8–10 reads: "Remember the Sabbath day, to keep it holy. Six days you shall labor, and do all your work, but the seventh day is a Sabbath to the LORD your God. On it you shall not do any work, you, or your son, or your daughter, your male servant, or your female servant, or your livestock, or the sojourner who is within your gates." The salient verse is verse 11: "For in six days the LORD made heaven and earth, the sea, and all that is in them, and rested on the seventh day. Therefore the LORD blessed the Sabbath day and made it holy."

Here we have the clear assertion that the universe was made "in six days." In the creation accounts of Genesis 1 and 2, we find the more detailed outworking of this work of creation in terms of days. In 1:3–5, we read: "And God said, 'Let there be light,' and there was light. And God saw that the light was good. And God separated the light from the darkness. God called the light Day, and the darkness he called Night. And there was evening and there was morning, the first day." In the rest of the account in Genesis, we read what takes place on the second day, on the third day, on the fourth day, and so on. The question is what is meant by the word "day" in the Genesis account. Throughout most of church history, it was understood that these verses of creation should be taken at face value and, as the text seems to suggest, that the work of creation was completed in six days, or six twenty-four-hour periods.

In the sixteenth century, when the Copernican Revolution took place and the telescope was invented and our capacity for understanding planetary motion and other aspects of astronomy increased, there were those who began to challenge the concept of a literal six-day creation. It's interesting that some of the finest Christian scholars of the sixteenth century, including the magisterial Reformers Martin Luther and John Calvin, ridiculed the Copernican theory of heliocentricity—namely, that the sun is the center of our solar system rather than the earth. They saw this new view coming out of the scientific community as an assault on the integrity of Scripture. It wasn't just the Roman Catholic Church that condemned Galileo and his associates for this view, but the Reformers also took a dim view on this question. Though for the most part Christians have made their peace with the idea of geocentricity (that the earth is the center of the universe), a few Christians still argue for geocentricity.

Part of the problem is that if the universe was created in six days, with Adam's being created at the end of the sixth day, followed by the rest of the biblical history of the generations of Adam, it doesn't seem to suggest a time span of human history that goes back millions of years. In the sciences of archaeology and anthropology, it seems that just about every six months there's a new discovery of remains of an older human ancestor. It seems that the dawning of the advent of man goes back about a million years every time they find a new skull fragment or something similar.

Modern forms of dating include geological methods, which are based in part on the stratification of the earth's crust, and carbon-14 dating. Perhaps most importantly, astrophysical methodologies are used to date the earth. This got quite technical and somewhat fascinating when triangulation emerged as a means of discerning the distances of stars from our solar system. We take as a matter of law now that the speed of light is 186,000 miles per second, and through modern ways of measuring distances and time, we find that the nearest star to our solar system is almost four and a half light-years away. A light-year is the distance that light travels in one earth year. To understand how far a light-year is, we can think about it in more earthly terms. Earth is 25,000 miles in circumference. Going around the world in eighty days is no difficult feat today, but light can travel around the world about seven and a half times in one second. Now imagine how far something traveling that fast could go in a year. The nearest star is so far away that the light traveling from it takes nearly four and a half years to get here. There are literally thousands of galaxies and multibillions and trillions of stars out there, and the light that we see today from far-distant stars started traveling millions and perhaps billions of years ago. It's more this astrophysical type of dating than any other thing, I think, that leads modern scientists to believe that the universe is far older than a few thousand years. It must go back 12 to 15 billion years to accommodate all this movement of light and so on.

A man named Hugh Ross wrote a book from a Christian perspective in which he advanced the theory of the old age of the earth from an astrophysical position. Many of you may be familiar with Professor Ross' book; he asked me to read the manuscript and write an endorsement for it. I wrote a somewhat benign endorsement, saying that it was a fascinating and interesting study, one that I thought was valuable for Christians to read and be engaged in, even though I didn't agree with a lot of things in that book. I have never in my life received anything like the volume of mail I received in protest to that endorsement.

I once saw a fascinating film about the 1980 eruption of Mount St. Helens. This eruption leveled many thousands of acres of land and turned gigantic trees into toothpicks. The scientists went in afterward and found something extremely interesting. They discovered a stratification of the earth's crust right around the base of the volcano that mirrored the stratification found elsewhere in the world. Such stratification was assumed from a uniformitarian geological perspective to have taken millions, if not billions, of years to produce. And this film showed that the same phenomenon could be produced in just moments by a catastrophic upheaval.

When we're talking about the age of the earth, however, we're dealing not simply with deductions from stratification of the earth but, as I said, with the carbon-14 phenomenon and the astrophysical dating phenomenon. Many different elements would seem to argue for an old earth.

Those who argue for a young earth have responses to each of these questions. In the early days of the debate, some rather bizarre arguments were used to offset the evidence of fossils that would indicate a long period of decay and compression and so on. I remember reading a theory some decades ago that when God created the universe, the devil sprinkled fossils throughout the layers of the earth to fool people and to distract them from believing in the trustworthiness of Scripture. The problem with that argument is that it is a possibility, hypothetically speaking, but it is incapable of being falsified. It's kind of like someone's arguing for poltergeists. A person might say that he believes in poltergeists, and somebody else might respond that the belief is invalid since we've never had any scientific, empirical verification of poltergeists. The first person might argue that the reason for the lack of evidence is that poltergeists never appear in the presence of scientists because they have a built-in allergy to scientists. How can you respond to an argument like that? You can't falsify it; nor can you verify it. Therefore, the argument is basically worthless. To say that Satan could have planted fossils when the Bible gives us no indication that Satan ever did such a thing and we have no reason to believe that he did is basically a worthless argument.

What is driving this debate over the age of the earth? Why are people so concerned about it? It goes back to the trustworthiness of Scripture. When I first started teaching in college many years ago, I was teaching in a Christian college where the class was so big that it had to be held in the chapel. The Bible that I used to teach the Old Testament was the pulpit Bible, and when I opened it up to Genesis 1:1 on the first day of class, at the top of the page of this Bible it said, "Genesis," and then in big print, "4004 BC." I knew, of course, that that date was nowhere to be found in the text of Holy Scripture. Why was it inscribed on the first page of this Bible? In the nineteenth century, Archbishop James Ussher tried to calculate the day of creation by examining the genealogical tables found in the Bible. Allowing so many years for each generation, Ussher calculated the date of creation by tracking back through these genealogical tables and concluded that the universe had been created in 4004 BC.

A whole generation of people were persuaded that this was true, and when scientists started saying that the earth was older than six thousand years, people felt a moral obligation to refute that claim in order to defend Ussher's date, a date that appears nowhere in sacred Scripture. Because there is no date of creation established in Scripture and every attempt to establish a date from Scripture is manifestly speculative, why do we spend all this energy trying to defend a particular date when the Bible doesn't give one? You might argue that Ussher could have been off by a few thousand years. Hebrew genealogies might be selective and have gaps, even gaps that are extensive and broad, which would account for some of the disparity. The Bible nowhere tells us that it is giving us a complete history of the human race. But even taking these factors into account would still not explain the difference between thousands of years and millions of years in dating the age of the earth.

Back to the question of six days. Again, one of the major considerations is the question of the age of the earth. At stake in many people's minds is the credibility and trustworthiness of sacred Scripture. There are those who believe that the authority of the Bible stands or falls with a young earth and with a recent date of creation.

When it comes to controversial and difficult questions like these, it's important to remember that when people in the church debate the issues, the debate is not between people who believe the Bible and people who don't believe the Bible. Those who are conservative and orthodox in their view of Scripture, those who hold to the inspiration, infallibility, and inerrancy of the Bible, are divided on this question. It's not a question of whether the Bible is true; rather, it's a question of what the Bible actually teaches.

3

Created in Six Days, Part 2

Genesis 1–2

In the last chapter, we were looking at the hot debate that has emerged over the dating of creation. Is the earth of relatively recent origin, or is it to be dated back twelve to fifteen billion years ago? This particular issue is closely related to the question of how we understand the reference to the six days of creation in Genesis. The questions are related but not totally identical to each other. As I previously mentioned, up until the Copernican Revolution in the sixteenth century, church tradition interpreted the days of creation in the opening chapters of Genesis to be historical twenty-four-hour periods. Since that time, there has been much debate in interpreting those verses.

Let's set the framework of the debate because it's sometimes hard to keep our eyes on what the real issues are. On the one hand are those people who are convinced that the Bible is simply the product of human ingenuity and insight and that the book of Genesis is an early Hebrew attempt to account for the world as we find it, a religious kind of mythological teaching similar in scope and style to other Near Eastern mythological cosmogonies, or theories of the origin of the universe, such as may be found in the *Epic of Gilgamesh* and other sources. Then there are those in the twentieth-century response against the radical skepticism of the nineteenth century who have taken a higher view of Scripture, but one that is still short of the orthodox view of divine inspiration and infallibility. For example, the Neoorthodox theologian Karl Barth allowed for the presence of legends and myths in the context of Scripture. Barth was once lecturing in the Netherlands, and during the discussion that followed, an attendee asked him this question with respect to the biblical account of the fall: "Did the serpent speak?" Barth's answer was this: "What did the serpent say?" In other words, Barth was saying that whether a real serpent actually spoke is irrelevant to the theological message of Scripture and that what does count is the message, what the serpent actually said, and what that meant for the story of Adam and Eve.

Of course, people in the Neoorthodox school often deny the historicity of the fall and the historical characters of Adam and Eve, not to mention the serpent. So this school of thought says that the Bible contains historical errors, errors of scientific evaluation, but what is important in Scripture is its redemptive theme and message. They argue that these details of history shouldn't be a concern to us. Yet from the more conservative perspective, there is a strong commitment to maintaining the traditional view of Scripture, one that strives to be faithful to the high view of Scripture that Jesus communicated and faithful to Scripture's claim to be the Word of God. The basic assumption is that if this is the Word of God, how can it make historical mistakes? The stakes of how we handle the question of the days of Genesis are indeed very high.

Also involved in this dispute is a question of hermeneutics, which is the science of biblical interpretation. Hermeneutics involves establishing and applying the fundamental rules of interpreting the written documents of Scripture—how words are to be handled, how word definitions apply, and so on. One of the subdivisions of hermeneutics that is important for biblical interpretation is *genre analysis*. *Genre* refers to the form or kind of literature that is being analyzed. For example, the rules for interpreting poetry are different from the rules that we use to interpret narrative history; this is because they are different forms of literature. So before we interpret a passage in the Bible or in any other book, we must first identify its literary form or genre.

The plot thickens when we ask whether we are to interpret the opening chapters of Genesis literally. When people ask me this question, my standard reply, which is somewhat shocking to many people, is simply: "Of course. What other way would we use to interpret the opening chapter of Genesis?

I think we're under obligation to interpret all of Scripture literally." Often when people ask me that question, they ask it with a negative tone: "R.C., you don't interpret the Bible literally, do you?"—as though I am uninformed, naive, and unsophisticated to interpret Scripture literally. I like to shock them and say, "Yes, I guess I'm that unsophisticated and naive as to do that." But then I realize that I have to interpret their question properly, and I often find that they have an understanding of what it means to interpret the Bible literally that is completely different from my own. To interpret the Bible literally is to interpret it according to the manner in which it is written. This is what the Reformers called the *sensus literalis*, or the "literal sense," of Scripture. It means that you interpret a noun as a noun and a verb as a verb, and you interpret poetry as poetry, epistles as epistles, historical narrative as historical narrative, and so on.

That throws us right back to this question of the literary form of these opening chapters of Genesis. A literal interpretation of Genesis is usually invoked to insist that the Hebrew word *yom*, which is translated "day," refers simply and exclusively to a single twenty-four-hour period. But there are other ways that this key word and the rest of the creation account are understood. We will look at three major possibilities.

The first possibility is that when the Bible speaks of creation in six days, it means six twenty-four-hour periods. Just as our day runs the cycle of twenty-four hours, morning and evening, that's exactly what was in view in the writing of creation. That is what the Bible intends to teach and has always intended to teach—that in six days, God completed the entire work of creation.

The second way that this is interpreted is by making use of the broader meaning of the term *yom* in Hebrew, which can refer not simply to a single twenty-four-hour period but to a much longer, though indefinite, period of time. For example, we use the term in a broader sense when we say, "Back in my day, we did things differently than today." In this instance, we're not making a distinction between twenty-four hours and six million years, but we are using the term "my day" to refer to "my generation" or "my youth." We do know that the term "day" can be and is used frequently in Hebrew in this broader, nonspecific sense. As a result, many have used that meaning to get away from some of the problems that the creation account is said to have with modern-day science. But the modern scientific "day" for the stages of creation would be days of billions of years, so really, little comfort can be drawn from this less-specific understanding of the Hebrew word for "day."

The third view is somewhat fascinating to me because it uses the term *yom*, or "day," to mean a twenty-four-hour period on the surface, though it uses the word in a dramatic, metaphorical way. In the middle of the twentieth century, a Dutch Old Testament scholar named Herman Nicolaas Ridderbos examined the literary form of these chapters of Genesis and concluded that they are arranged in a peculiar literary form that is more akin to drama than to normal historical narrative. Ridderbos helped to develop the *framework hypothesis*, which has had various modifications since. The hypothesis suggests that Genesis speaks of the creation of the universe in six definitive stages, like a six-act play. The literary framework for this dramatic figurative description of creation is marked by the phrase "there was evening and there was morning, the [*nth*] day." It is believed that these references to days are references, more or less, to acts in a six-act drama or a figurative description of the work of creation. Some people object that this approach already involves a rejection of biblical authority. Yet this hypothesis, whether it's a sound one or an inaccurate one, is designed to ask what the literary form is that we're dealing with in the opening chapters of Genesis.

This view is fascinating because it is not based on a low view of Scripture. It simply is struggling with the proper identification of the literary format and structure of Genesis, which is not a simple matter to discern at first glance. For example, elements in the opening chapters of Genesis seem very much consistent with normal, regular historical-narrative literature. When the Bible describes the garden of Eden, for example, it locates Eden with respect to certain known historical rivers such as the Euphrates, and references to real geographical places are normally a sign of historical-narrative literature. Characters in this event include Adam and Eve, who are later included in genealogical tables in both the Old and New Testaments, which is a strong argument in favor of understanding that the biblical writers believed that Adam and Eve were real, historical people. On the surface, there are clear elements of normal historical-narrative literature to which the normal laws of literary analysis apply.

On the other hand, in Genesis the garden of Eden is described as containing a Tree of Life. Where do we find a Tree of Life in anybody else's garden?

This is a kind of fantasy element that is found right alongside historical-narrative elements. That the creation account mixes elements in this way has led some scholars who have a high view of Scripture to conclude that the account belongs to a unique literary genre.

The point of the framework view is that the universe did not happen as a cosmic accident but that the universe was clearly created by a sovereign God. That affirmation is without any ambiguity. Furthermore, it was done in stages that took place successively within a framework of six acts. The literary device for indicating those stages, according to the framework hypothesis, is the occurrence of "evening" and "morning" at the end of each day. Holding to this position does not necessarily mean abandoning the authority of Scripture.

The debate over the days of creation involves trying to square an affirmation that is made by sacred Scripture with judgments that emerge from scientific inquiry. We've seen this in the past—how we're convinced, as Christians, that the Bible itself teaches that God reveals His truth not only through the Scripture but also through nature and through what we call general revelation. The revelation that God gives in one place never contradicts the revelation He gives in another place. Whatever He reveals through nature will be consistent with what He reveals in the Bible, and what He reveals in the Bible will be consistent with what He reveals in nature. Sometimes our understanding of what God reveals in nature is incorrect and is corrected by a clearer understanding of what is taught in Scripture. It can also happen the other way—sometimes we acknowledge that what God gives to us from nature corrects a misunderstanding of the Bible, which I think is what happened with the Copernican Revolution in the sixteenth century. We must always be open to the possibility that our understanding of Scripture should be corrected by our understanding of God's revelation in nature.

4

The Sons of God

Genesis 6

One of the most prominent biblical scholars to come out of Germany in the twentieth century was Rudolf Bultmann, who gave a massive critique of the Scriptures. He argued that the Bible is filled with mythological references and that for it to have any significant application to our day, the biblical interpreter must first demythologize the text of Scripture. Bultmann's major concern was with the New Testament narratives, particularly those that include records of miracles, the occurrence of which he deemed impossible. The same issue has been raised with the Old Testament Scriptures. Yet more conservative scholars have examined the genre of material in the Old Testament and have argued that the biblical literature is already demythologized compared to the literature of other ancient religions. The mythological narratives that we're familiar with from the ancient Greeks and Romans have elements that are obviously mythological, such as the birth of Athena from the head of Zeus.

In those mythological histories, we frequently read about the sins of the gods and goddesses and their mating with human beings. Mating between gods or goddesses and human beings is part and parcel of the substance of ancient mythology. The Old Testament contains a text that some of the critics argue is a clear example of the same sort of mythological narrative that is found, for example, among the ancient Greeks. The highly debatable passage is in Genesis 6:

When man began to multiply on the face of the land and daughters were born to them, the sons of God saw that the daughters of man were attractive. And they took as their wives any they chose. Then the LORD said, "My Spirit shall not abide in man forever, for he is flesh: his days shall be 120 years." The Nephilim were on the earth in those days, and also afterward, when the sons of God came in to the daughters of man and they bore children to them. These were the mighty men who were of old, the men of renown.

The LORD saw that the wickedness of man was great in the earth, and that every intention of the thoughts of his heart was only evil continually. And the LORD regretted that he had made man on the earth, and it grieved him to his heart. So the LORD said, "I will blot out man whom I have created from the face of the land, man and animals and creeping things and birds of the heavens, for I am sorry that I have made them." But Noah found favor in the eyes of the LORD. (vv. 1–8)

This narrative is more like a preface, an introduction, to the more major narrative that follows it—namely, the account of the flood by which the human race was eradicated from the face of the earth, except for the family of Noah. It is concerning this preparatory section, however—where we read of the intermarriage between the sons of God and the daughters of men—that the charge of blatant mythology is brought against the Old Testament text.

The assumption that is made in the mythological interpretation of Genesis 6 is that the phrase "sons of God" refers to angelic beings. Notice that the Old Testament does not say explicitly that there was sexual intercourse between angels and human women. It talks about intercourse between "the sons of God" and "the daughters of man." The assumption that passage refers to angels is based on instances in the Scriptures when angels are called the sons of God (e.g., Job 1:6; 38:7). That is certainly a possible inference that could be drawn from this text in Genesis 6. The question is, Is it a necessary inference? I would say that it is not and that the text doesn't necessarily teach the idea of such interaction between angels and human beings. To understand this, we have to look at the broader application of the phrase "sons of God."

There are ways in which the term "son of God" is used, as I said, for an angel. It is also used in a somewhat different sense for Christ. When Jesus engaged in debates with the Pharisees, much of the focus was on Christ's claim of sonship in relation to the Father. Conversely, Jesus called the Pharisees sons of the devil during an argument over His ability to make men free (John 8:12–59; see v. 44). The Pharisees protested and didn't understand the need for the freedom of which Jesus spoke. They argued that they were in bondage to no man because they were the children of Abraham (v. 39). Yet Jesus' response was that they were children of the one they obeyed. That's when He called them children of Satan because they were followers and disciples of Satan rather than of God.

The concept of sonship in the Scriptures is not always linked to some kind of biological relationship but is often defined in terms of a relationship of obedience. Christ was uniquely the Son of God in His being, according to His divine nature, but even according to His human nature He was uniquely the Son of God in the sense that He was pleasing to the Father because of His perfect obedience. All this is to say that the title "son of God" or "sons of God" may refer biblically to those who are in a relationship of obedience to God. Is it possible that in Genesis 6, we're reading of the intermarriage between those who were from a pattern of obedience to God and who wed those women who were pagans in their orientation? We have then a description of mixed marriages between believers and unbelievers that would pollute the whole society. It's not far-fetched to conclude that that is what the author of Genesis is talking about in light of the context of the early chapters in Genesis.

To see that context, we have to back up and realize that after the fall in Genesis 3, the Bible then records the first example of homicide when Cain killed his brother Abel (ch. 4). What then follows is a rapid expansion or broadening of human sinfulness. Furthermore, what follows after the narrative of the first homicide is a brief summation of two lines of families, the first being the descendants of Cain (4:16–24) and the second being the descendants of Seth, the son born to Adam and Eve after Abel's death (4:25–5:32).

In Genesis 4:16–24, we get a brief survey of the history of the family of Cain:

Then Cain went away from the presence of the LORD and settled in the land of Nod, east of Eden. Cain knew his wife, and she conceived and bore Enoch. When he built a city, he called the name of the city after the name of his son, Enoch. To Enoch was born Irad, and Irad fathered Mehujael, and Mehujael fathered Methushael, and Methushael fathered Lamech.

And Lamech took two wives. The name of the one was Adah, and the name of the other Zillah. Adah bore Jabal; he was the father of those who dwell in tents and have livestock. His brother's name was Jubal; he was the father of all those who play the lyre and pipe. Zillah also bore Tubal-cain; he was the forger of all instruments of bronze and iron. The sister of Tubal-cain was Naamah.

Lamech said to his wives:

"Adah and Zillah, hear my voice;
 you wives of Lamech, listen to what I say:
I have killed a man for wounding me,
 a young man for striking me.
If Cain's revenge is sevenfold,
 then Lamech's is seventy-sevenfold."

Lamech is recorded in Scripture as the first polygamist, which involves a departure from the ordinance of marriage that God gave in the garden. This genealogy of Lamech presents the building of cities in an arrogant way; Cain names the city he built after his son. Then we have this dreadful account of what is known as the "Sword Song" of Lamech, in which Lamech is rejoicing in his murderous, vengeful use of the sword in hatred. So we get the idea that this line of people is a line of proliferation of human wickedness.

What follows is in Genesis 4:25–26: "And Adam knew his wife again, and she bore a son and called his name Seth, for she said, 'God has appointed for me another offspring instead of Abel, for Cain killed him.' To Seth also a son was born, and he called his name Enosh. At that time people began to call upon the name of the LORD." Then in chapter 5, we get further elaboration of the line of Seth, which included such righteous men as Enoch, Methuselah, and Noah.

So we have two genealogies in these early chapters of Genesis—one is the line of Cain and the other is the line of Seth. The line of Cain reads like a rogues' gallery of wickedness in the Old Testament, and the line of Seth is a line of amazing godliness marked by Enoch, Methuselah, and Noah. These two lines existed side by side, one being godly, following the Lord, while the other one expanded in wickedness and ungodliness. Chapter 5 ends with the following statement: "After Noah was 500 years old, Noah fathered Shem, Ham, and Japheth." The very next verse is the introduction of the multiplication of the people on the earth and the daughters that were born to them. This is when we hear of the sons of God marrying the daughters of men.

Many Hebrew scholars believe that chapter 6 describes not the intermarriage between angels and human women but the intermarriage between the descendants of Cain and the descendants of Seth. One line had been growing in godliness and the other one had been intensifying in wickedness. Suddenly this is disrupted when the two lines come together; now everybody is caught up in this relentless pursuit of evil, and the desires of their hearts are only wicked continually. Only Noah is left from the sons of God—that is, those who are obedient to God. Because of Noah's obedience, God grants Noah grace and spares him as God decides to destroy the rest of mankind.

The problem in Genesis 6 of the apparent intermarriage between the sons of God and the daughters of men serves a broader purpose for us, and that's to warn us to be very careful about the inferences that we draw from Scripture that are not necessarily warranted. The descriptive terms "sons of God" and "daughters of man" do not give us license to make the assumption of interaction between heavenly beings and earthly beings. We have to be very careful when we look at a difficult text like this to see how the same language is used in the broader context of all Scripture. It's a very important principle of interpretation to interpret Scripture by Scripture.

5

The Hardening
of Pharaoh's Heart

Exodus 7

One of the hard sayings of the Bible that is among the most debated in the life of the church has to do with God's hardening of Pharaoh's heart. This particular hard saying raises all kinds of questions about God's relationship to evil and about human responsibility. Let's look at one of the references to this hardening:

> And the LORD said to Moses, "See, I have made you like God to Pharaoh, and your brother Aaron shall be your prophet. You shall speak all that I command you, and your brother Aaron shall tell Pharaoh to let the people of Israel go out of his land. But I will harden Pharaoh's heart, and though I multiply my signs and wonders in the land of Egypt, Pharaoh will not listen to you. Then I will lay my hand on Egypt and bring my hosts, my people the children of Israel, out of the land of Egypt by great acts of judgment. The Egyptians shall know that I am the LORD, when I stretch out my hand against Egypt and bring out the people of Israel from among them." (Ex. 7:1–5)

This is not the only reference in the book of Exodus to God's hardening the heart of Pharaoh. After chapter 7, we read about the succession of plagues that God sends on the land of the Egyptians—the frogs and gnats, the river turning to blood, and so on. What happens is a kind of oscillation whereby, after one plague comes upon the people of Egypt, Pharaoh relents for a season and grants permission for the Israelites to leave, but usually with restrictions or stipulations. When it seems as though the Israelites are going to be liberated, we read again the refrain "Pharaoh's heart was hardened." Pharaoh changes his mind and tells Moses that the Israelites can't go out into the wilderness to serve their God. He continues to enslave them until another plague is sent upon the Egyptians. He then begins to melt and to be inclined to allow the Israelites to leave, but then we read again that God hardens Pharaoh's heart.

At first glance, it almost seems as though God is mercilessly playing with Pharaoh as a puppet in His hand, hardening his heart and then judging him for the actions that he takes as a result of this hardened heart that was given to him by God. How are we to deal with this difficult concept in Scripture? In the first place, we must see that the Scriptures explicitly ascribe the hardening of Pharaoh's heart to God, not only in terms of describing what takes place over and over through these various plagues, but initially, before the plagues even begin, in terms of God's announcing to Moses that that's exactly what He's going to do. God said that He wanted Moses to be as God to Pharaoh, to be His spokesman. God was empowering Moses with miracles, and Aaron would be the one to deliver the message to Pharaoh. God wanted Moses to know that Pharaoh was not going to listen because God would be hardening his heart.

We usually dance around this sort of thing and say that what really happened was that Pharaoh hardened his own heart and that God had nothing to do with it. This line of thinking supposes that it would be unjust or unbecoming of God to coerce a human being to do evil and then punish that human being whom He has coerced. That would be an act of great evil. I hope we can see and feel the intensity of this dilemma that we face as a result of these descriptive terms. Yet this view does not do justice to the biblical account. We must understand that the Scriptures make it clear that the ultimate causal agent for the hardening of Pharaoh's heart is almighty God.

Whatever the text means by God's hardening Pharaoh's heart, it is not the hardening of the heart of a holy, righteous, innocent man. The hardening of Pharaoh's heart, however it is accomplished, is a judgment of God on a person who is already recalcitrant in his soul and at enmity with his Creator. He's already living as a despot, as a tyrant, enslaving people cruelly and unjustly, living a daily life of radical disobedience to the heavenly King to whom he is always accountable. Pharaoh, in a word, is a sinner, and a sinner who is behaving in a very sinful manner. That is the case even before there's any discussion about God's hardening his heart. What that means is this: when God hardens Pharaoh's heart, the act of divine hardening is a judgment of God on someone who is already sinful. It is a judgment that is completely consistent with what is said throughout Scripture about how God will judge the wicked.

In the final account of the last judgment in the book of Revelation, the judgment on the sinners who are impenitent is simply this: "Let the evildoer still do evil" (Rev. 22:11). Elsewhere, the Scriptures describe one way of God's judgment on people as His giving them over to Satan. In addition, we read in the New Testament that one of the ways that God distributes His common grace to the world is by restraining human sin. Under His divine government of world history, God puts restraint on evil by not allowing us to be as wicked as we could possibly be.

If we were to make a list of the most diabolical, the most wicked people ever to walk on the stage of history, who would be on that list? When I ask people to list the most evil people in history, the same names come up over and over again. One person who makes everybody's list of bad guys is Adolf Hitler. Another one who ranks high is Joseph Stalin. Nero is also a common answer. Let me just take these three figures—Nero, Hitler, and Stalin—and ask what they have in common. One was Roman, one was German, and one was Georgian. They were from different times and different places and they ruled over different forms of government, but they were each the head of a nation. They all had virtually supreme authority vested in the offices that they held. Who was able to restrict Nero in his wickedness? Who was able to restrain Hitler from the unmitigated evil he perpetrated on the world? Who could limit Stalin's slaughter of millions of people in Ukraine and elsewhere? In America, while we've had some rogues who have ruled over us on more than one occasion, our system of government was designed to have a system of checks and balances so that no single individual can wield too much power.

From the lessons of history comes Lord Acton's aphorism that "power tends to corrupt, and absolute power corrupts absolutely." That statement is not absolutely true. It's only relatively true. It is true only when applied to human beings; God and God alone has absolute power, and there's no corruption in Him whatsoever. In any case, we have with these earthly figures an enormous level of power and authority by which they could do pretty much what they wanted without the fear of restraint. The ones who restrained Hitler were the leaders of other nations. He ran into the restraining influence of Winston Churchill, Franklin D. Roosevelt, and the Allied forces who finally defeated him in his desire to expand his own wickedness. What I'm saying is simply this: when we give a catalog of the great villains of history, they tend to include people who had enormous levels of political power and authority, which means that they had very little, if any, human restraint on them.

Pharaoh was the most powerful man on the face of the earth in his day. The earthly might of the entire Egyptian Empire was vested in this one man. The only real significant restraint on Pharaoh was God. The only One more powerful than Pharaoh was God. The only reason that the Israelites who were enslaved did not suffer even worse crimes and atrocities than they did was the restraining hand of God. When we study the doctrine of divine providence, we see that God, in His power and in His government, rules over all earthly kingdoms and over all earthly individuals. He raises nations up and He brings nations down, so Pharaoh couldn't rule for five seconds in Egypt were it not for the sustaining governing power of the providence of God. In an ultimate sense, Pharaoh could do only what he was permitted to do by the sovereign Governor of the universe.

God, the text tells us, is the One who hardens Pharaoh's heart, and He does it for a reason. It is plain throughout the exodus account that the principal reason that God hardens the heart of Pharaoh is so that the people He is redeeming, this people that He is liberating and gathering to Himself to be His chosen people, to be a holy nation, might understand unambiguously that salvation is of the Lord and only of the Lord. Lest the Israelites think that they've accomplished their redemption through their own efforts or even through the good graces of Pharaoh, God makes it abundantly clear that it is God who is performing this miraculous work of redemption.

At this point, one might be thinking that God's purpose in all this may have been good, with a redemptive end in view, but it still leaves the question, How can God's forcing Pharaoh to commit evil and then punishing Pharaoh for committing that evil be justified? The key idea in that question is *force*, which leads us to ask *how* God could harden the heart of Pharaoh. He could do so in at least two distinct ways, one of which would be utterly inconsistent with what the Scriptures teach us about the character of God, and the other of which would be perfectly consistent with what the Scriptures teach us elsewhere about the character of God.

Let's look first at the one that would be inconsistent with the character of God: God could harden Pharaoh's heart by intervening in his soul to create fresh evil in his heart and then punishing him for doing what comes naturally. That raises all kinds of problems concerning God's justice and seems to make Him the author of evil, an idea that is repugnant to Scripture.

The second possibility is the one that is consistent with the teachings of the rest of Scripture. Martin Luther argued that in the hardening of Pharaoh's heart, God did not come in and directly or immediately create fresh evil in Pharaoh's heart. Rather, He removed His common grace from Pharaoh—He removed the restraints—because the tender grace of God was the only thing that had kept Pharaoh's heart from being any harder than it already was. For God to make Pharaoh's heart harder, He didn't have to create fresh evil in that heart. All He had to do was to take His mercy away, remove the restraints, take the leash off, step aside, and let Pharaoh do whatever he wanted to do.

This is consistent with what Scripture states elsewhere regarding the awful judgment of God by which He gives people over to their sin—which, incidentally, is what is indicated in the final act of church discipline when a person is excommunicated. The person is delivered to Satan and exposed to the temptation of the evil one. The hedge of divine protection, such as that which surrounded Job before Satan was given permission to have at him, is removed. This is what happens every time someone is excommunicated, and this makes excommunication such a dreadful thing to comprehend. However dreadful, it is consistent with God's orientation toward sinners who want to sin, who want the restraints removed, who want the leash untied, who are begging to be free, ultimately free, to express the wickedness that is stored up in their hearts. When God judges them, He is saying: "OK, if you want evil without reservation, I'll let you have it. I'll remove My restraint. I'll remove My common grace and abandon you to your own evil inclinations and disposition." That's exactly what God did with Pharaoh. To put it simply, He let Pharaoh be Pharaoh.

6

Strange Fire

Leviticus 10

The story of Aaron's sons Nadab and Abihu, who were slain rapidly and decisively by God, is of abiding consternation for many of God's people. The account is found in Leviticus 10: "Now Nadab and Abihu, the sons of Aaron, each took his censer and put fire in it and laid incense on it and offered unauthorized fire before the LORD, which he had not commanded them. And fire came out from before the LORD and consumed them, and they died before the LORD" (vv. 1–2).

Aaron was the first high priest of the Israelite nation, so he was consecrated to a holy vocation. Because Aaron was the high priest, the head of the Aaronic priesthood, it was significant that his sons would follow in his footsteps. God had selected from among the twelve tribes of Israel the tribe of Levi to be consecrated to the work of ministering in the tabernacle/temple. The family of Aaron, from among the Levites, was ordained and set apart for the priesthood. We read in Leviticus 10 that two of Aaron's sons, Nadab and Abihu, each took his censer, a kind of vessel that was used to burn incense before the Lord, and offered what the book of Leviticus calls, in the English Standard Version, "unauthorized fire." Some translations read "strange fire" or "alien fire," while other versions use "profane fire."

What is profane fire? The word *profane* is used in our vocabulary to refer to that which is less than sacred, less than holy. When we speak of profanity, we often mean using words in a way that is unacceptable to God. Martin Luther called the church, the ministry, and the priesthood "profane." This sometimes causes people to wonder why a Reformer would speak of the ministry as *profane*. Luther was using the term in a way that was much closer to its original meaning than the way we use it today. *Profane* comes from the Latin *profanus*, meaning "outside the temple." When Luther said that the church had a profane ministry, he meant that the church is called to come out of the temple and into the world, that the world is the arena of ministry for the Christian community. He didn't mean that the church should be pagan or ungodly, irreligious or unholy. When Leviticus 10 uses the term, it means it in a way that is closer to our contemporary understanding, in the sense of "unholy." The offering was truly "outside the temple" in that it was not fit for the temple because it had not been purified or consecrated.

On the surface, it seems that this is a case of cruel and unusual punishment. The sons of Aaron obviously violated some detail of the prescription that God had set forth for the offering of incense in the Holy Place, and for this seemingly minor misdeed or innovation they were not simply admonished or rebuked but were killed instantly. Confronted with this account, we must ask, Is this really what happened? Is this an accurate, inspired account of divine judgment on the sons of Aaron? Or, as critics have suggested, is this part of the primitive, naive ancient Hebrew explanation for natural events that they interpreted mystically or theologically?

Immanuel Velikovsky was somewhat of a maverick in the scientific world; he wrote two best-selling books in which he challenged some of the pet theories of modern science. In one book, he did a detailed critical analysis of the anomalies that are unresolved in uniformitarian geology. In another book, he proposed a hypothesis based on a careful study of the folklore, mythology, and traditions of nations around the world. He discovered that their ancient writings contained some clear recurring themes about astronomical phenomena. Velikovsky's working assumption was that ancient myths were attempts to explain phenomena in the world around them that they didn't understand scientifically. In his judgment, real historical events and natural phenomena were behind the primitive and crude attempts of ancient peoples to explain their world. For example, stories about enormous deluges are found in various ancient mythological accounts, which led Velikovsky to conclude that there must have been some kind of dramatic flood in the ancient world to which these accounts are attesting.

Velikovsky's primary concern, however, was an astronomical perturbation that must have been catastrophic in scope because so many ancient peoples recorded a heavenly body's coming close to the earth, having a large tail and looking something like a huge comet. He noticed that allusions to Venus are absent in a certain period in ancient astrology and then suddenly occur again later. He concocted a theory about what would happen if a huge object were to come close enough to Earth to enter its atmosphere and what kind of catastrophic upheaval there would be. He attributed, for example, the pillar of smoke and the pillar of fire in the wilderness experience of the Israelites to the tail of this object that had come close to the earth and that the Jews wandered all around following.

Velikovsky further speculated that this object, with all its smoke and fire, would have dropped a kind of flammable liquid onto the planet. That liquid would have seeped into the layers of the earth, and this was his explanation for why the Middle East is so rich in petroleum. He made his appeal from this text in Leviticus to support his theory. He said that this flammable substance that was being dumped on the planet had been discovered by a couple of young priests who decided to experiment with it on the altar. When they did, it blew up in their faces and killed them. It had nothing to do with divine judgment; it was simply a natural event caused by a drastic mistake.

Velikovsky's theory is interesting, but our concern is how the Bible itself understands this event. Even if this event did happen as a result of Nadab and Abihu's offering petroleum on the altar, we still have an example of the judgment of God because, under God's providence, these men were doing something that they were not supposed to be doing. They were offering strange fire, whatever it was.

When the fire consumed Nadab and Abihu and they were killed on the spot, Aaron was greatly displeased. He had given his life in devotion to God, and his sons who had come into the priesthood made one mistake at the altar and God took their lives. You can just hear Aaron in his distress coming to Moses and asking: "What's going on? What kind of repayment is this? I serve the Lord day and night, and He kills my sons for a peccadillo, for a small offense." I'm reading between the lines here, of course, because all Scripture says is that Moses spoke to Aaron. I'm assuming that Aaron went to Moses very distressed and Moses reminded Aaron of what the Lord had spoken: "Among those who are near me I will be sanctified, and before all the people I will be glorified" (v. 3). Moses, speaking to Aaron, said: "Aaron, do you remember what God said when He consecrated you in the first place? Do you remember the law He delivered regarding the behavior of the priesthood, that one nonnegotiable regarding the behavior of the priesthood? Almighty God insists that He will be regarded as holy by anyone who draws near to Him."

Sometimes the accounts of the Old Testament, particularly in terms of historical narrative, are shockingly brief, as profoundly deep and moving experiences are recorded for us in the barest of terms. Though it's dangerous to speculate, it's difficult to avoid with accounts like this one that are so abbreviated, and we try to reconstruct them in our own minds. We see the vast understatement that is so characteristic of the Scriptures at the end of verse 3: "And Aaron held his peace." That's the end of the story. The fact that he held his peace suggests that before Moses reminded him of the terms of the priesthood, Aaron was not at all in an irenic frame of mind. Then Moses reminded him and Aaron held his peace. It essentially means that he shut up. The argument was over, and there was nothing left to debate.

To understand what Moses said more fully, let's go back to the book of Exodus. In chapter 19 of Exodus, just before the giving of the Ten Commandments in chapter 20, God spoke to Moses and told him to command the people to prepare a fast and to spend some time consecrating themselves before the day comes when God will come to the top of the mountain and meet with Moses personally. The narrative tells us that there was lightning and thunder and a deep cloud on the mountain. God had made a law that nobody apart from Moses was allowed to approach the mountain or set foot on the mountain. If anyone touched the mountain, he was to die. In that context we read these words: "And the LORD said to Moses, 'Go down and warn the people, lest they break through to the LORD to look and many of them perish. Also let the priests who come near to the LORD consecrate themselves, lest the LORD break out against them.' . . . And the LORD said to him, 'Go down, and come up bringing Aaron with you. But do not let the priests and the people break through to come up to the LORD, lest he break out against them'" (19:21–22, 24). At this founding event of the nation of Israel, the giving of the law, God applied the laws of consecration, which were then repeated when He established the priesthood. He warned the Israelites that if they were not consecrated and they violated the consecration, God would break out against them. Nadab and Abihu violated the holy law of the priesthood, and when they did, God killed them to remind Israel of the sanctity of the presence of God.

In the life of the church today, we are no longer encouraged to have a healthy fear of God. We seem to assume that the fear of the Lord is something that belongs exclusively to the Old Testament and is not to be a part of the life of the Christian. Yet fear in the Old Testament involves not simply a trembling before God's wrath and vengeance but a sense of reverence, a sense of awe, before His holiness. Even though the wall of partition has been removed and though we are living on this side of the cross, the fear of the Lord is still the beginning of wisdom (Prov. 9:10). The mark of an unbeliever is having no fear of God before his eyes.

God hasn't changed. He is still an all-consuming fire. When we come into His presence, we are to come as children and we are to come as those who have been reconciled. But there is to be a godly fear that still respects the One with whom we are dealing.

7

Holy War

Deuteronomy 20

Modern people, particularly in the Western world, have great difficulty in conceiving of any war that could be considered holy. Yet in Judaism and in Christianity, we have to deal with the record of the Old Testament in which we read of God's commanding His people in the conquest of Canaan to be involved in such a war. This raises questions about the credibility of the Old Testament sources.

Some modern commentators look at the biblical accounts of holy war and say one of two things. First, some say that the God of the Old Testament is a different God from the one we meet in the pages of the New Testament because Christ comes to us as the Prince of Peace, whereas Yahweh is sometimes described in the Old Testament narratives as a vengeful God, even so vengeful as to institute such a thing as holy warfare. Other modern commentators assert that the command to engage in holy war is an example that shows that the Old Testament Scriptures are not really the Word of God but are simply the religious viewpoints and insights of primitive people who, at times, could be barbaric in their behavior and who tried to justify their barbarism by appeals to divine sanctions.

Let's look at some of the texts that are concerned with the concept of holy war in the Bible. In Deuteronomy 20:1–4, we read:

"When you go out to war against your enemies, and see horses and chariots and an army larger than your own, you shall not be afraid of them, for the LORD your God is with you, who brought you up out of the land of Egypt. And when you draw near to the battle, the priest shall come forward and speak to the people and shall say to them, 'Hear, O Israel, today you are drawing near for battle against your enemies: let not your heart faint. Do not fear or panic or be in dread of them, for the LORD your God is he who goes with you to fight for you against your enemies, to give you the victory.'"

In this passage, God gives a challenge to His people not to be afraid in the face of military conflict because He promises not only to be with them in their battle but to fight for them to save them or rescue them from defeat.

Later on in this same chapter is some of the material that is so difficult for us to handle:

"When you draw near to a city to fight against it, offer terms of peace to it. And if it responds to you peaceably and it opens to you, then all the people who are found in it shall do forced labor for you and shall serve you. But if it makes no peace with you, but makes war against you, then you shall besiege it. And when the LORD your God gives it into your hand, you shall put all its males to the sword, but the women and the little ones, the livestock, and everything else in the city, all its spoil, you shall take as plunder for yourselves. And you shall enjoy the spoil of your enemies, which the LORD your God has given you. Thus you shall do to all the cities that are very far from you, which are not cities of the nations here." (vv. 10–15)

Notice that in this aspect of the warfare, there is first of all an offer of peace to the cities that are in the way of the advancing Israelite troops, and if a city surrenders, the people are to give tribute to Israel and become enslaved to Israel, but the people are not to be destroyed. God commands Israel, however, that if a city resists the Israelite advance and refuses to come to terms of peace, Israel was to lay siege to the city and to kill every male in the city and plunder its goods.

The text continues:

"But in the cities of these peoples that the LORD your God is giving you for an inheritance, you shall save alive nothing that breathes, but you shall devote them to complete destruction, the Hittites and the Amorites, the Canaanites and the Perizzites, the Hivites and the Jebusites, as the LORD your God has commanded, that they may not teach you to do according to all their abominable practices that they have done for their gods, and so you sin against the LORD your God." (vv. 16–18)

In the case of these regions that are to be invaded, the cities of the Canaanites and so on, God institutes what is called the *herem* in the Old Testament. *Herem* refers to things that are "put under the ban"—that is, wholly devoted to the Lord, generally by total destruction. A city's being placed under "the ban" meant that God required everything in the city to be utterly annihilated: men, women, and children. This included not only the soldiers but the civilian population also, and their goods were to be destroyed as well. We have here a claim to a divine mandate not only to be engaged in warfare but to be engaged in the absolute destruction of the conquered city or nation. You can see why people gasp at this idea and why the people of Israel became an object of fear, as we see in the case of Rahab and the citizens of Jericho, who had heard of the devastation of cities and nations under the leadership of Moses and later Joshua (see Josh. 2).

How can we explain this? Let's suppose for a second that this isn't simply the expression of primitive barbarians who were trying to appeal to religious sanctions for their ambitions of world conquest. Rather, let's suppose that this is the veritable Word of God. How does the Christian who believes that the Old Testament Scriptures are indeed the truth of God understand the rationale behind the institution of the *herem*? Several things need to be said about that. Earlier in the book of Deuteronomy, some rationales are given for these instructions:

"And when the LORD your God brings you into the land that he swore to your fathers, to Abraham, to Isaac, and to Jacob, to give you—with great and good cities that you did not build, and houses full of all good things that you did not fill, and cisterns that you did not dig, and vineyards and olive trees that you did not plant—and when you eat and are full, then take care lest you forget the Lord, who brought you out of the land of Egypt, out of the house of slavery. It is the Lord your God you shall fear. Him you shall serve and by his name you shall swear. You shall not go after other gods, the gods of the peoples who are around you—for the Lord your God in your midst is a jealous God—lest the anger of the Lord your God be kindled against you, and he destroy you from off the face of the earth." (6:10–15)

The author goes on to say that, in the first place, the conquest of Canaan is to be understood as the fulfillment of the promise that God had given centuries earlier to Abraham and to his descendants. God had promised Abraham that he would be the father of a great nation, that he would inherit the land, that his descendants would be as the stars of the sky and as the sand on the seashore, and that God would be his God; in addition, this Old Testament covenant included a promise of land (Gen. 12:1–3). God makes it clear to Abraham and to his descendants that an inflection point in history is being reached and that the reason that God rescues the Israelites out of bondage in Egypt and gives them this promised land is not because they deserve it (see Gen. 15:16). God makes it clear that His people are just as sinful as these pagan idolaters who are already inheriting the land. But God calls Abraham out of paganism, out of idolatry, and reveals Himself to him and gives a special measure of His grace to him. Again, we have to understand that it is grace that Abraham receives from God and that this covenant promise that God makes to Abraham and to his seed is not based on anything that they deserve or any merit on their part. God reminds the Israelites, when they're about to enter Canaan, that He's going to give them a land to use that they did not clear, establish, cultivate, or build. God is going to give them houses that they didn't build for them to live in. He's going to give them cisterns that they didn't dig and vineyards that they didn't plant so that they can use them for their own refreshment. He's reminding the Israelites that they didn't do any of these things; these things have been done for them. God reminds them that when they go in there and enjoy the fruits of somebody else's labor, they are not to allow that to puff them up with pride, lest they forget the gift of the Lord their God.

That's part of the rationale behind the *herem* that we see described further in Deuteronomy 7 with these instructions:

"When the LORD your God brings you into the land that you are entering to take possession of it, and clears away many nations before you, the Hittites, the Girgashites, the Amorites, the Canaanites, the Perizzites, the Hivites, and the Jebusites, seven nations more numerous and mightier than you, and when the LORD your God gives them over to you, and you defeat them, then you must devote them to complete destruction. You shall make no covenant with them and show no mercy to them. You shall not intermarry with them, giving your daughters to their sons or taking their daughters for your sons, for they would turn away your sons from following me, to serve other gods. Then the anger of the LORD would be kindled against you, and he would destroy you quickly. But thus shall you deal with them: you shall break down their altars and dash in pieces their pillars and chop down their Asherim and burn their carved images with fire.

"For you are a people holy to the LORD your God. The LORD your God has chosen you to be a people for his treasured possession, out of all the peoples who are on the face of the earth. It was not because you were more in number than any other people that the LORD set his love on you and chose you, for you were the fewest of all peoples, but it is because the LORD loves you and is keeping the oath that he swore to your fathers, that the LORD has brought you out with a mighty hand and redeemed you from the house of slavery, from the hand of Pharaoh king of Egypt. Know therefore that the LORD your God is God, the faithful God who keeps covenant and steadfast love with those who love him and keep his commandments, to a thousand generations." (vv. 1–9)

Why are these campaigns commanded by God called "holy wars"? It's important to understand that the word *holy* has two different meanings. The basic meaning of the term *holy* is "apartness, otherness, separateness, transcendence." When we say that God is "holy," we mean that God transcends all creatures, that He is *other* from all created things, that He is a higher order of being than anything that we find in this world. The secondary meaning of the term *holy* is "pure." When God calls His people to be holy even as He is holy, He's saying two things that could be combined into one: "First of all, I want you, as My holy people, to be different, other, apart from what commonly constitutes pagan humanity. I want that apartness to be demonstrated in purity, in righteousness, in obedience to My law, so that My people will reflect and mirror who I am, will be followers of Me, will obey My statutes, and will walk according to My laws and be a royal priesthood, a light to all nations." God chose, from all the nations of the world, a nation that was the least of all nations to become His people, to be the focal point of His light, of His grace, and of His mercy; to be a light to the nations. Abraham is chosen to be a blessing. He is blessed by God in order that through him the whole world will be blessed.

We could consider the first holy war to be the flood during the days of Noah, when God marshaled His military power of nature and annihilated nearly the whole population of the world as an act of judgment. When we see the invasion of Canaan, God makes it clear that He is using Israel as His arm of vengeance, as His instrument of cleansing and purging the land. Judgment is falling on the Canaanites because of their manifest wickedness and idolatry and paganism. God told Israel to go in there; to level the place; to tear down the altars, destroy their idols, get rid of all the remnants of their religious institution; and to purge the land of the people. God didn't want the Israelites intermarrying with them because, before long, syncretism would take place. This is, however, exactly what happened because Israel didn't consistently apply the *herem* and its purpose of holiness. The holy war was to sanctify the land, to sanctify a nation, in order that the mercy of God, the love of God, and the righteousness of God would be made manifest.

I've often wondered what would happen to us if God would declare holy war on our own nation. We sometimes smugly assume that anytime we are in conflict with other countries or nations, God must be on our side. During the pinnacle of the Cold War, President Ronald Reagan referred to the Soviet Union as the "evil empire," and the assumption was that if there ever was a conflict between the Soviets and the Americans, God would clearly be on our side. That's a very dangerous assumption to make because we saw in the Old Testament what happened to Israel. God was on Israel's side in the initial invasion, but when Israel disobeyed, God raised up nations more wicked than Israel to punish Israel. This is what caused the prophet Habakkuk and other prophets in the Old Testament so much consternation. They wrestled with how God could allow Israel to fall captive to the Babylonians and others. We need to be careful in this age that we do not tacitly assume that God will always be on our side. He is on the side of those who obey Him.

8

Rahab's Lie

Joshua 2

In the book of Joshua, we meet a person who does some very strange things for which she is remembered in the annals of church history. One of the most remarkable things she does is to tell a lie that is quite effective. I'm referring to the harlot Rahab, whose story is recounted in the second chapter of the book of Joshua. Rahab is remarkable enough that she is listed in the roll call of the heroes and heroines of the faith in Hebrews 11. It's significant that the person who tells this lie is elevated to such a role of heroism in the New Testament.

We read these words in Joshua 2:1: "And Joshua the son of Nun sent two men secretly from Shittim as spies, saying, 'Go, view the land, especially Jericho.'" Before we get to Rahab and her lie, allow me to comment on some of the background.

Joshua is now the general of the Lord's army. He is the successor to Moses, and he is leading the conquest of the land of Canaan, the land that God had promised to their fathers. Before chapter 2 begins, God had already promised Joshua that He would give to Joshua every place where he put his foot (1:3). We might ask why Joshua would bother to undergo this risky business of sending two of his elite soldiers into this hostile territory. Risking their lives seems unnecessary, since God had already decreed that Joshua would be triumphant. We have to understand a principle that we find throughout Scripture: even though God has decreed certain things to come to pass and we know that His plans will be fulfilled, we are still given the responsibility to diligently do the things through which God brings those events to pass. Even in the life of the church, we know that He will gather His people from the four corners of the world, but we're still called to proclaim the gospel. We could just rest back and say, "God, all Your people are going to be redeemed anyway, so I might as well sleep in tomorrow." That is a posture of disobedience toward the Lord God. Even though Joshua is given the promise of victory by God, he is still required to act as a diligent commander.

Part of that diligent process is to assess the strength of the enemy stronghold that Joshua is going to be moving against. Earlier, when spies had been sent into Canaan, they came back with a pessimistic report, information about giants in the land, and doubts about whether they were going to be able to achieve victory. Only two of the spies were faithful and returned from their mission with a report of a land flowing with milk and honey. Their eyes weren't on the giants or on the strength of the enemy but were on the promise of God and the opportunities that were there. These two faithful spies, who were then granted the privilege of entering the promised land, were Caleb and Joshua. Joshua selected two men who he knew were like him, faithful spies, and sent them to spy out this land and provide an intelligence report.

"And they went and came into the house of a prostitute whose name was Rahab and lodged there" (Josh. 2:1). The Bible doesn't say why they went to Rahab's house, but we know this: her house was part of the wall of the city of Jericho. It was a marvelous place to provide the spies with a vantage point to see what was going on in the whole city. Furthermore, if there's any place in an ancient city where foreigners would not be obtrusive or stand out by their presence, it would be the house of a prostitute. Prostitutes, then as now, have a tendency to cater to those in commercial centers where tradesmen are in and out of town, in ports of call where sailors are disembarking from ships, and so on; there would have been a certain anonymity in a place where prostitution happened. From a strategic military point of view, this would be a good location to maintain secrecy. There's no reason to assume that these spies were lecherous men looking for an occasion to be with a prostitute.

"And it was told to the king of Jericho, 'Behold, men of Israel have come here tonight to search out the land'" (v. 2). The strategic reason for their visiting the house of Rahab was to help conceal them and to keep their cover, and obviously it didn't work because very quickly the word got to the king of Jericho that these strangers, who were identified as Israelites, were present in the city. Keep in mind that the army of Israel was camped fourteen miles away, and it was a huge throng of fierce warriors camped out there. It is likely that the king of Jericho already knew the whereabouts of the army of Israel because that kind of thing was communicated very rapidly in the ancient world. You don't hide a whole army that close to a walled city.

> Then the king of Jericho sent to Rahab, saying, "Bring out the men who have come to you, who entered your house, for they have come to search out all the land." But the woman had taken the two men and hidden them. And she said, "True, the men came to me, but I did not know where they were from. And when the gate was about to be closed at dark, the men went out. I do not know where the men went. Pursue them quickly, for you will overtake them." But she had brought them up to the roof and hid them with the stalks of flax that she had laid in order on the roof. So the men pursued after them on the way to the Jordan as far as the fords. And the gate was shut as soon as the pursuers had gone out. (vv. 3–7)

Rahab is a Canaanite, so her allegiance is supposed to be to the king of Jericho. The first thing Rahab is guilty of is civil disobedience. She disobeys her king. The second thing she's guilty of is telling a manifest falsehood to the representatives of the king. Listen again to what she says: "True, the men came to me." So far, so good; she's telling the truth. "But I did not know where they were from." That's a lie. "And when the gate was about to be closed at dark, the men went out." That's another lie. "I do not know where the men went." That's another lie. "Pursue them quickly, for you will overtake them." That's not a lie; it's just intentionally fraudulent advice. Based on the evidence in this narrative, we know that Rahab lied. We also think that she is morally bankrupt, since she was involved in the practice of prostitution, she was involved in civil disobedience, she was a traitor to her own country, and she was a liar of the highest magnitude in these circumstances. How can a person like that be considered an archetype of a godly woman?

How are we going to make sense out of this kind of behavior and the exaltation that the Scriptures give to her as a great heroine of the faith? Before I try to answer that directly, let me continue with the narrative to the section of the text that I call the "sermon on the roof":

> Before the men lay down, she came up to them on the roof and said to the men, "I know that the LORD has given you the land, and that the fear of you has fallen upon us, and that all the inhabitants of the land melt away before you. For we have heard how the LORD dried up the water of the Red Sea before you when you came out of Egypt, and what you did to the two kings of the Amorites who were beyond the Jordan, to Sihon and Og, whom you devoted to destruction. And as soon as we heard it, our hearts melted, and there was no spirit left in any man because of you, for the LORD your God, he is God in the heavens above and on the earth beneath. Now then, please swear to me by the LORD that, as I have dealt kindly with you, you also will deal kindly with my father's house, and give me a sure sign that you will save alive my father and mother, my brothers and sisters, and all who belong to them, and deliver our lives from death." And the men said to her, "Our life for yours even to death! If you do not tell this business of ours, then when the LORD gives us the land we will deal kindly and faithfully with you."
>
> Then she let them down by a rope through the window, for her house was built into the city wall, so that she lived in the wall. And she said to them, "Go into the hills, or the pursuers will encounter you, and hide there three days until the pursuers have returned. Then afterward you may go your way." The men said to her, "We will be guiltless with respect to this oath of yours that you have made us swear. Behold, when we come into the land, you shall tie this scarlet cord in the window through which you let us down, and you shall gather into your house your father and mother, your brothers, and all your father's household. Then if anyone goes out of the doors of your house into the street, his blood shall be on his own head, and we shall be guiltless. But if a hand is laid on anyone who is with you in the house, his blood shall be on our head. But if you tell this business of ours, then we shall be guiltless with respect to your oath that you have made us swear." And she said, "According to your words, so be it." Then she sent them away, and they departed. And she tied the scarlet cord in the window. (vv. 8–21)

In a sense, the plot thickens because it now seems, as her sermon on the roof indicates, that the reason that she's helping these men and concealing them is that she is terrified of the wrath of the Jewish army that is encamped fourteen miles away. She mentioned hearing about the savage exploits of the Israelite army and how her people's hearts melted when they understood that they were next on the army's list. She was doing this kindness to the spies by hiding them so that they would protect her and her family from the inevitable onslaught that's going to come with the invasion and siege of Jericho. It now seems that the motive for her trying to help these spies of Israel is purely self-serving, for herself and for her family.

If we listen carefully to the words that she uses in this discourse, however, she makes it clear that she believes in the God of Israel, that she is a believer in the Lord. We don't know how that came to pass, but it was probably a recent occurrence. The significance of this, which we might miss in passing over it, is that the peoples of the ancient Near East had their national gods, but they did not believe that their gods were the only gods that existed. They believed that there was a god for the Canaanites, a god for the Philistines, a god for the Assyrians, a god for the Babylonians, and so on. They were henotheists, meaning that they worshiped one god in particular as their supreme god among many other gods, and that one god was seen to be over one ethnic group or one national territory. Yet Rahab acknowledges that the God of Israel is not merely a territorial or ethnic deity; rather, He is the God of heaven and earth, the Creator, the Most High God. She gives a remarkable confession of faith, in essence a confession of the doctrine of the Israelite beliefs, and reveals her Israelite faith at that point.

It's also remarkable how Rahab takes charge of the whole situation. These two elite soldiers have come into her house, and she has to mother them, hurry them up to the roof, hide them under these stalks of flax, and tell them to be quiet. All the while, she takes care of the representatives of the king of Jericho, sending them on a wild-goose chase. Rahab is taking a great risk in telling the lies that she does and in deceiving the representatives of the king.

The ethical question we face is whether her lie was justified. There is disagreement on this point. Some great theologians in church history have argued that Rahab is called a great saint despite her lie, not because of it, but that if she really believed in divine sovereignty and the providence of God, she would have told the truth and then trusted God to intervene and save the spies. I disagree. I think that her lie was not only morally acceptable but also heroic.

To understand this view, we must go to the broader ethical teaching of Scripture with respect to the sanctity of truth, which is that lying is wrong because it violates God's righteousness and justice. Moral theologians have historically understood that at the heart of biblical justice is the principle of giving people their due. We reward those who have earned a reward, and we punish those who have earned punishment; that's what justice is about. The principle used in understanding these circumstances is that we are always obliged to tell the truth to whom the truth is due. We are always to tell the truth when righteousness and justice require us to tell the truth. But we are not required to tell the truth to someone who has no right to it.

In this circumstance, Rahab's duty is to protect these representatives of God from the wickedness of the king of Jericho. As a result, her civil disobedience and her lie are both justified because she is obeying the mandate she has from God. She is not to participate in the destruction of God's people in this circumstance. This situation is very similar to that of people who hid Jews in their homes during World War II. They were doing the ethical thing by concealing the truth from the wicked who were seeking to destroy the Jews. It's the same sort of thing that the midwives did when they lied to Pharaoh about the destruction of the Jewish babies, and we see that God pronounced His benediction on them (see Ex. 1:15–22). Rahab was being courageous and righteous in protecting the godly from the unrighteous king of Jericho.

One of the little side narratives of this account is the pact that Rahab made with the spies. She wanted to make sure that her family would be spared when the Israelites came to attack the city. The spies warned her, however, that if some of her family stayed outside, the Israelites wouldn't be able to know who they were, and her family members' blood would not be on the spies' hands if they were killed in the conflict. The spies told Rahab to make sure to keep her family in her house. Further, there needed to be some kind of sign so that the troops of Israel would know that her house was not to be destroyed. The spies told Rahab to put a scarlet cord in the window. We read that she led them out of her house down the wall with a rope. She knew it would be days, if not weeks, before the army came.

As soon as she had given the spies further guidance on where to go and how to hide, she obeyed the terms of the covenant that she had made with them by putting the scarlet cord in the window. How fitting that the sign of her redemption was marked in red. How fitting that it was the same sort of sign that had been placed on the doorposts of the homes of the Israelites when the angel of death passed over, because the judgment of God was to pass over the household of Rahab when the army saw the sign of God in her window.

9

Blind Eyes
and Deaf Ears

Isaiah 6

The sixth chapter of Isaiah contains the record of Isaiah's call. Isaiah has a vision in which he sees God seated on His throne surrounded by the heavenly angels, the seraphim, who are singing the refrain "Holy, holy, holy." Isaiah's initial response to this vision is to curse himself, saying: "Woe is me! For I am lost; for I am a man of unclean lips, and I dwell in the midst of a people of unclean lips; for my eyes have seen the King, the Lord of hosts!" (v. 5). God then instructs an angel to bring a live coal from the altar and cleanse Isaiah's mouth. After that, God speaks in verse 8: "Whom shall I send, and who will go for us?" And it's at that point that Isaiah volunteers for ministry.

This is the occasion of Isaiah's call to the office of prophet, when he is set apart by God, consecrated to this sacred task, and is spiritually anointed for this mission. When God asks, "Whom shall I send, and who will go for us?" Isaiah answers: "Here I am! Send me" (v. 8). The moment that Isaiah volunteers for this mission of representing God as His spokesman, God delivers to Isaiah a hard saying.

God tells the prophet in verses 9–10: "Go, and say to this people: 'Keep on hearing, but do not understand; keep on seeing, but do not perceive.' Make the heart of this people dull, and their ears heavy, and blind their eyes; lest they see with their eyes, and hear with their ears, and understand with their hearts, and turn and be healed." What an enormous burden God places on Isaiah. He sends Isaiah to a people who are rebellious, who are obstinate, and who have no inclination whatsoever to turn themselves to the things of God or to delight in the Word of God. Therefore, God sends Isaiah not to open their eyes but to shut their eyes, not to open their ears but to close their ears.

We usually think of the mission of the preacher as one designed for spiritual renewal and spiritual awakening. Yet here Isaiah is being sent not to awaken people but to put them into a stupor, a torpid state, by which they will not be awakened to the things of God.

In the New Testament, we hear a similar type of message that comes to us from the lips of Jesus. In Matthew 13, we read Jesus' parable of the sower. In this parable, Jesus tells of a sower who sows seed, and some of the seed falls on the good earth, some in stony places, some among thorns, and some on good soil. Jesus concludes in verses 8–9: "Other seeds fell on good soil and produced grain, some a hundredfold, some sixty, some thirty. He who has ears, let him hear." Implicit in this statement is that there are those who don't have ears to hear. For those who do not have ears to hear, our Lord does not invite or command them to hear. That provokes a question with us as soon as we hear it, and it certainly provoked a question in those who heard Jesus make that statement originally.

In verse 10, we read this: "Then the disciples came and said to him, 'Why do you speak to them in parables?'" Many people assume that Jesus speaks in parables for the same reason that any other speaker uses illustrations—that is, to clarify His message and to make it easier for people to understand what He's trying to communicate. The parables are meant to make difficult notions or ideas plain. So when the disciples ask, "Why do you speak to them in parables?" we would expect Jesus to respond, "I speak in parables so that you can have an easy way to understand My teaching." But that's not what He says. Here is His answer:

> "To you it has been given to know the secrets of the kingdom of heaven, but to them it has not been given. For to the one who has, more will be given, and he will have an abundance, but from the one who has not, even what he has will be taken away. This is why I speak to them in parables, because seeing they do not see, and hearing they do not hear, nor do they understand.

Indeed, in their case the prophecy of Isaiah is fulfilled that says:

> """You will indeed hear but never understand,
>   and you will indeed see but never perceive."
> For this people's heart has grown dull,
>   and with their ears they can barely hear,
>   and their eyes they have closed,
> lest they should see with their eyes
>   and hear with their ears
> and understand with their heart
>   and turn, and I would heal them.'" (vv. 11–15)

After finishing this quotation from Isaiah 6, Jesus adds: "But blessed are your eyes, for they see, and your ears, for they hear. For truly, I say to you, many prophets and righteous people longed to see what you see, and did not see it, and to hear what you hear, and did not hear it" (Matt. 13:16–17). This is an amazing teaching from our Lord. He answers the question "Why do You teach in parables?" by saying, "The parable enlightens, illustrates, illumines, elucidates, and clarifies the truth of what I am teaching for those to whom it has been given to understand." That is, "To My elect, whom God has given ears to hear and eyes to see, I speak in parables because understanding of these spiritual things has been given to them."

The Bible in various places states that certain spiritual truths can only be discerned spiritually, and that only through the assistance of the Holy Spirit as the supreme illuminator may certain truths be understood. At Caesarea Philippi Jesus asked the disciples, "Who do you say that I am?" and Peter responded, "You are the Christ, the Son of the living God" (Matt. 16:15–16). Jesus declared: "Blessed are you, Simon Bar-Jonah! For flesh and blood has not revealed this to you, but my Father who is in heaven" (v. 17). That's a hard saying because it's tied to the hardest saying of all, the doctrine of election, which states that God gives to some a special grace by which He changes the disposition of their hearts. He gives us ears to hear and eyes to behold what we would not naturally see or hear. Likewise, Jesus said to Nicodemus, "Unless one is born again he cannot see the kingdom of God" (John 3:3), indicating that the unregenerate person simply can't see certain things about the character of God. Have you ever wondered, in the midst of your enjoyment of the beauty and the sweetness of Christ, why your unbelieving friends seem to be so indifferent or even hostile toward that which is the most important, meaningful, precious thing in all your life?

I remember once doing an evangelism call at a home where two young ladies lived, and one was openly hostile to Christianity. I was trying to go through the Scriptures with her and to explain the basic essence of the gospel to this woman, and she kept interrupting and saying: "Look, I've heard that a thousand times. My uncle was a minister." I said, "Well, could it possibly harm you to hear it just one more time?" I asked her for permission to finish, she allowed me to do so, and I left. Six months later, this woman showed up in a new members class at the church where I was serving. The other minister asked her, "What led you to want to come and become a member of this church?" She told the story of our visit to her home that night. To be honest with you, I'd forgotten about it, but she told how she had been hostile, belligerent, and totally closed to the hearing of the gospel, and she related how I had asked her to let me finish sharing with her. As soon as we walked out the door, she went back to her bedroom and burst into tears, got on her knees beside her bed, alone, and embraced Christ as her Savior. She remarked: "I thought I had heard it, but I had never heard it before. It never penetrated before." That's not because I was more articulate or more persuasive than her uncle or the other people who had told her these things, but that seed had been planted before on stony ground. It had been tossed among thorns. But in the meantime, God had done a work in this woman's heart that prepared the soil for the seed to be planted and to bring forth its fruit to germinate into life. She had been given "ears to hear."

Jesus is saying, as He harks back to Isaiah, that the gospel, the preaching of the Word, is a two-edged sword. Nobody can hear the Word of God and remain neutral. Nobody can be indifferent to the truth of God. Either you hear it and respond to it willingly, being pleased by the sweetness of it, or you reject the Word of God and shut it out from your life.

Isaiah is called to deliver the message of God to a nation that had heard His Word proclaimed over and over and over again. The Israelites had the oracles of God, and they despised the truth of God. God said: "Isaiah, you go out there and you preach, but I'm sending you to deaf ears and to blind eyes, and the message that you preach will actually have the effect on these people of hardening their hearts. I'm sending you out on a mission of judgment, not a mission of rescue."

The coming of Christ provoked the same kind of crisis. When He came to those who did not have ears to hear, He spoke in parables to hide the kingdom of God from them because it didn't belong to them. The kingdom of God was being offered to Christ's people, and in a sense, the same parable that disclosed the mystery of the kingdom of God to those people was at the same time hiding the kingdom from those who were indisposed toward it. That's the crisis of the Word of God.

Isaiah responded to the call in the same way that any of us might have. When Isaiah hears that he's supposed to go on a mission like this, he says, "How long, O Lord?" (Isa. 6:11). God replies with an answer: "'Until cities lie waste without inhabitant, and houses without people, and the land is a desolate waste, and the LORD removes people far away, and the forsaken places are many in the midst of the land. And though a tenth remain in it, it will be burned again, like a terebinth or an oak, whose stump remains when it is felled.' The holy seed is its stump" (vv. 11–13). Do you see the message here? Now God is saying: "Isaiah, I know this is tough. I know that the vast majority of the people to whom you declare the things of God will reject them. The message will fall on deaf ears. But I have reserved for Myself a remnant." Here we have the introduction of the Old Testament concept of the remnant, the holy seed that God has preserved for Himself.

When you hear the preaching of the gospel, do you get it? Does it get through to you, or does it bounce off you? Are you impervious to it? Does it bore you, make you yawn, make you fall asleep? Can you not wait for the sermon to be over? Or are you the kind of person who delights in the Word of the Lord, can't get enough of it, wants to learn more and more because it gets sweeter and sweeter by the moment? That's what I hope is your experience.

10

The God of Prosperity and Evil

Isaiah 45

We're now going to turn our attention to another hard saying from the prophet Isaiah, and this saying is hard both in the sense of trying to understand its meaning and in the sense of its apparent severity.

> "For the sake of my servant Jacob,
>> and Israel my chosen,
> I call you by your name,
>> I name you, though you do not know me.
> I am the LORD, and there is no other,
>> besides me there is no God;
> I equip you, though you do not know me,
> that people may know, from the rising of the sun
>> and from the west, that there is none besides me;
> I am the LORD, and there is no other.
> I form light and create darkness;
>> I make well-being and create calamity;
> I am the LORD, who does all these things." (Isa. 45:4–7)

The King James Version's translation of verse 7 reads, "I form the light, and create darkness: I make peace, and create evil." That translation of the text raises eyebrows because it explicitly says, "I . . . create evil." This causes many people to ask: "What does this mean? I thought that we were not supposed to believe that God is the author of sin or that God creates evil."

When I was a graduate student in Europe studying the question of the origin of evil, my professor at the Free University of Amsterdam, G.C. Berkouwer, made mention of what he called the biblical *a priori*. The phrase *a priori* is a technical term that is frequently found in the discipline of philosophy, but it's not often used in ordinary speech. Something that is *a priori* is "innate," "fundamental," or "foundational." The word comes from the Latin, which basically means "before experience." Its antonym is *a posteriori*, which means "after experience." When we talk about something *a priori*, we're talking about a basic idea. The Declaration of Independence spoke about inalienable rights that we learn about from nature, and so on, which sort of fell back on the thinking of the British philosophers and, even before that, the rationalists such as René Descartes, who was seeking for what he called "clear and distinct ideas." In a sense, Descartes was searching for *a priori* truth, truth that is self-evident. That might sound familiar—"we hold these truths to be self-evident." That would be an *a priori* truth, basic and controlling to everything that you think.

When I was in this course in Europe and Professor Berkouwer spoke about "the biblical *a priori*," he said that the single biblical *a priori* that is to govern all our thinking, that which is foundational to all religious understanding, is this: "God is not the author of evil." If that's so foundational, how do you deal with a passage in Scripture that is translated by the words "I am the LORD, and there is none else. I . . . create evil" (Isa. 45:6–7, KJV)? It certainly seems, at least on the surface, that Isaiah has little time for Professor Berkouwer's biblical *a priori* because Isaiah seems to deny it clearly and emphatically by saying that God creates evil.

There are two ways that we need to approach this text as we seek to understand what is being said. But before we look at these two ways, we must qualify the so-called biblical *a priori*. When the biblical *a priori* is declared to be that God is not the author of evil, that means that God Himself never does that which is evil. How do we relate that to the idea of God's creating evil? If it's evil for God to create evil, then God could not create evil. Yet we live in a world that God has created, and there is clearly evil in the world. So we know, at least, that God has created beings who have the capacity for evil. Satan was able to do evil, or he wouldn't have done it; Adam and Eve were capable of sin, or they wouldn't have sinned.

It's manifestly obvious that God has created beings who were capable of falling into sin and of performing sinful actions, but that's still not the same thing as saying that God Himself created evil. The biblical record indicates that God created Satan and that Satan was originally a good angel, but he became evil. Likewise, Adam and Eve were created good, and then they later became evil. But still, God stands above and beyond and over and behind all this activity.

With that in mind, the first thing we have to see about this text in Isaiah 45 is that when it speaks of God's creating evil, it's not talking in the first instance about moral evil. The Old Testament word for "evil" has at least seven different nuances. Usually when we use the word "evil," we're talking about moral evil—sin—while the Scripture speaks of badness or evil in other categories as well. It speaks of natural disasters such as sickness, floods, hurricanes, and earthquakes, which indicate physical evil. These are done not by villainous people but by impersonal nature. When nature erupts in an earthquake, nobody starts screaming that Mother Nature has done something sinful, yet we use that word "bad" or "evil" with respect to such a calamity. A famine also is a physical calamity, but it's not a manifestation of some particular person's moral corruption. Anything that is bad to the Hebrew can be called "evil."

The kind of evil in view in Isaiah is relatively easy to discern. Several literary devices are commonly found in the Wisdom Literature of the Old Testament, the chief of which is *parallelism*. In parallelism, certain statements are placed alongside each other in some sort of relationship, so there are different kinds of parallelisms. In *synonymous parallelism*, the same idea is communicated in two different ways. Here's an example: "The LORD bless you and keep you; the LORD make his face to shine upon you and be gracious to you" (Num. 6:24–25). That's saying the same thing, but in two different ways. In *antithetical parallelism*, a contrast is stated in a poetic way, so that something positive is stated, followed by its negative. That's what we have here in Isaiah 45.

We read in verse 7, "I form light and create darkness." There is the clear contrast between God's work of creativity in terms of making both the light and the darkness. Light and darkness stand in contrast to each other. In this text, we actually have a form of synonymous parallelism, with two verses that are basically saying the same thing, but the thing that they are saying is a matter of contrast, so this could also be identified as antithetical parallelism. The first line of verse 7, "I form light and create darkness," says that God does both— He makes the light and He makes the darkness, even though these two stand in contrast. In the next line, a similar statement is made by God, which would make it synonymous parallelism, but at the same time, it's also a statement of contrast. Notice what the contrast is: "I make well-being and create calamity." Other translations might say, "I make peace, and create evil" (KJV) or "I bring prosperity and create disaster" (NIV).

The ESV translation reads, "I make well-being and create calamity." The translators here are trying to get at the force of the original Hebrew. While some translators use "evil" on that second side of the structure, the type of evil that is in view is not moral evil, but it is that evil that is in direct contrast to well-being, peace, or prosperity, so what Isaiah is saying here as a spokesman for God is that God brings blessing and He brings curse. He brings good times; He brings bad times. He brings peace; He also brings conflict. He brings weal; He also brings woe. He brings well-being; He brings calamity.

It's not that the text is saying that God does moral evil or creates moral evil. It is saying, however, that God is ultimately the author of all that comes to pass. What this passage is communicating, beloved, is the sovereignty of God over the entire creation. The refrain "I am the LORD, and there is no other" (v. 6) gets at this idea: "I am responsible for the whole of the creation, for the whole of human history. My divine, sovereign providence stands over all human events. I bring the abundant harvest. I will also bring the famine. I bring the sunny day. I also bring the storm. I bring the arid desert. I also bring the flood."

Isn't it interesting that even our insurance policies have clauses for those things that are called *acts of God*? At least the insurance underwriters have some sense of sound theology because the idea of the Hebrew is that all of life, all of nature, is under the authority and the government of almighty God.

It is important for us to make the distinction that theologians have historically made between primary and secondary causality. Primary causality means that the ultimate source of all power, the power to do anything in the universe, resides with God. In a sense, I can't even do moral evil apart from the power of God. That's a hard saying in and of itself. I don't have the power to do anything apart from God, who is the foundation of all being and all power. The author of Acts says, "In him we live and move and have our being" (17:28). That doesn't mean that God makes me sin. I'm the one who wants to sin, but I can't even execute my sin unless God in His sovereignty decides not to stop me. I can't draw a breath apart from His sovereign power. My acting to sin is an instance of secondary causality, and secondary causality is real causality. I really do act when I sin, but I could not do so were it not for the sovereign power of God.

That's the lesson that Isaiah is conveying here. He's not trying to teach us that God is bad. He's trying to teach us that God is sovereign. He's not trying to give us a lesson on the origin of sin here or even on the origin of evil. That's another vexing question for another time, but this message is designed to teach us of the unique governing authority of God.

"For the sake of my servant Jacob, and Israel my chosen, I call you by your name" (Isa. 45:4). God is saying: "You wouldn't have a name, you wouldn't have a destiny, there wouldn't be a nation of Israel if it were not for Me. I am the One who chose you. I am the One who formed you. I am the One who named you. I am the One who redeems you. I am the One who gives you blessing. I am the One who gives you judgment. I am the One who brings you prosperity. I am the One who brings you calamity. I am the Lord, and there is no other."

The sovereignty of God, indeed, stands above and behind every single thing that ever happens. That in itself is hard for us to swallow because lots of things happen to us that are genuinely tragic in their real-life circumstances. But when we understand that the sovereignty of God stands above and behind even the tragedies of our lives, we have no reason to curse the darkness or to think that this casts a shadow over the goodness of God, but we have a reason for the greatest hope and greatest comfort we can experience. When God exercises His government of the universe, in His sight there are no tragedies. It's because God stands sovereign over all human circumstances that the

Scriptures can say, "And we know that for those who love God all things work together for good, for those who are called according to his purpose" (Rom. 8:28). When we are called according to His purpose and are His children, even the tragedies, as tragic as they may be in their earthly manifestation, ultimately redound to our good and to the glory of God.

11

Jeremiah's Temple Speech

Jeremiah 7

Jeremiah's temple speech is one of the most famous speeches that was ever given by a prophet in the Old Testament. The account is found in Jeremiah 7: "The word that came to Jeremiah from the LORD: 'Stand in the gate of the LORD's house, and proclaim there this word, and say, Hear the word of the LORD, all you men of Judah who enter these gates to worship the LORD. Thus says the LORD of hosts, the God of Israel: Amend your ways and your deeds, and I will let you dwell in this place. Do not trust in these deceptive words: "This is the temple of the LORD, the temple of the LORD, the temple of the LORD""" (vv. 1–4).

Jeremiah is instructed by God to go to the gates of the Jerusalem temple. There at the entrance to the temple, God requires Jeremiah to preface his sermon by saying, "Hear the word of the LORD." Jeremiah begins by calling the people to solemn attention in a way that is reminiscent of the *Shema* in Deuteronomy 6:4. God is about to make a divine pronouncement that is of extreme importance.

Jeremiah announces, "Thus says the LORD of hosts, the God of Israel: Amend your ways and your deeds, and I will let you dwell in this place" (Jer. 7:3). There's already something strange about the message. What do you mean, we should amend our ways and our deeds, and God will let us dwell in this place? Isn't this the God of Abraham, Isaac, and Jacob? Is this not His city? Haven't we received the holy city of Jerusalem as the promise of God unto all generations?

The Israelite people, at this point in their history, were utterly convinced that Jerusalem was indestructible. Other cities may fall, other cities may be conquered in battle, but never Jerusalem. Its walls were formidable, but more important than the physical protection of the city was the divine protection. This was God's city. This was the capital established by David. It was unthinkable to the Israelites that anything could ever happen to disrupt or disturb the peace of Jerusalem. But there's something strange in the opening words of Jeremiah's speech. It contains a conditional: "Amend your ways and your deeds, and I will let you dwell in this place." If the Israelites don't amend their ways, something dire, something dreadful, something unspeakable could happen to Jerusalem.

Jeremiah goes on to say, "Do not trust in these deceptive words: 'This is the temple of the LORD, the temple of the LORD, the temple of the LORD'" (v. 4). In Isaiah 6, Isaiah the prophet has his vision of the heavenly sanctuary, where he sees the seraphim surrounding the throne of God, singing in antiphonal response to the glory of God, singing the *Trisagion*, the "three times holy," saying, "Holy, holy, holy." The importance of God's holiness is highlighted by the angelic host's repeating the word "holy" three times.

One of the literary devices or techniques that the Jews used to indicate emphasis was repetition. The normal way of calling attention to something extremely important was saying it twice, just as Jesus prefaces some of His most important teaching to His disciples by saying, "Truly, truly, I say to you" (e.g., John 1:51). But on a few extremely rare occasions in Scripture, something is deemed so important that it is elevated to the third degree, the superlative degree; it's said three times. It is significant that the angels do not simply declare that God is "holy" or even "holy, holy" but say that He is "holy, holy, holy." In the book of Revelation, when the vials and the bowls of God's wrath are poured out on the world, an angel cries out, "Woe, woe, woe" (8:13). The threefold announcement of doom indicates an extraordinary measure of divine judgment.

Why does Jeremiah make use of this literary device of repetition to the third degree? He is emphasizing the radical degree of the hypocrisy of the people who think that by empty repetitions, by saying over and over and over again, "This is the temple of the LORD, the temple of the LORD, the temple of the LORD," they have done something holy or meritorious or they now have magical power to sustain them and to protect them against the judgment of God.

Notice what Jeremiah calls these words that were repeated by the people: "deceptive words." This is strange because they're not lies; this was indeed the temple of the Lord. Jeremiah calls them deceptive words because they express the truth, but they were not proclaiming the truth truthfully. Rather, these words had become lying words in the mouths of those who were bringing false worship into the presence of God.

Just because a church is a church does not mean that it's a church. That may sound ridiculous, but I mean that it can be a church outwardly, but if it doesn't obey the Lord of the church, it's no longer really a church. We can't put our trust in the building or even in the institution. As important as those things may be, God is most interested in our faith in Him and our obedience to Him. If we are disobedient to God, we cannot take refuge in our church membership or our church affiliation.

Jeremiah continues, still speaking for God, "For if you truly amend your ways and your deeds, if you truly execute justice one with another, if you do not oppress the sojourner, the fatherless, or the widow, or shed innocent blood in this place, and if you do not go after other gods to your own harm, then I will let you dwell in this place, in the land that I gave of old to your fathers forever" (Jer. 7:5–7). Then the next word should also get our attention—"Behold." It means "look here!" It's a call to attention. Here, Jeremiah says, "Behold, you trust in deceptive words to no avail" (v. 8).

You talk about a hard saying—to come to the people of Israel in the very front of the temple and say to them, "The creeds that you're professing and the liturgy that you're using have now become dishonest expressions and words that are empty, words that are vain, words that are deceitful, words that are hypocritical. That kind of language and those words are futile; they are useless words that cannot profit." These people were talking the talk, but they were not walking the walk.

"Will you steal, murder, commit adultery, swear falsely, make offerings to Baal, and go after other gods that you have not known, and then come and stand before me in this house, which is called by my name, and say, 'We are delivered!'—only to go on doing all these abominations? Has this house, which is called by my name, become a den of robbers in your eyes? Behold, I myself have seen it, declares the LORD" (vv. 9–11). This anticipates Christ's reaction in the New Testament when He cleansed the temple. God is saying, centuries before Jesus cleansed the temple, that the people had already defiled the temple. They go through the ritual on the Sabbath day, they go through all the machinations of religion, but their lives are pagan during the rest of the week. They are religious, but they are not faithful. Their religion is phony. So God says: "I know what you people are doing. You have taken My house, the house that is called by My name, and turned it into a place that mocks what it's about." The question is, What is God going to do about it?

This is where we really come to the hard part:

> "Go now to my place that was in Shiloh, where I made my name dwell at first, and see what I did to it because of the evil of my people Israel. And now, because you have done all these things, declares the LORD, and when I spoke to you persistently you did not listen, and when I called you, you did not answer, therefore I will do to the house that is called by my name, and in which you trust, and to the place that I gave to you and to your fathers, as I did to Shiloh." (vv. 12–14)

Shiloh was one of the earliest places of worship in Israel. It had been the central sanctuary where people came to offer their sacrifices and to worship God until Jerusalem became the capital city under David. It then became the central sanctuary where the temple was built. At this point in history, Shiloh was rubble. Shiloh had been utterly devastated and destroyed. Nothing was left but garbage and heaps of stone.

God is saying: "You think your confidence is in this building, is in the religious trappings here? Go to Shiloh. I destroyed it because of the wickedness of the people of Israel, and I'll do the same to Jerusalem." This was the hardest message that any prophet ever had to announce to the people of Israel, that Jerusalem was going to be destroyed. Jeremiah taught it, Isaiah taught it, and all the false prophets denied it until the year 586 BC, when the Babylonians came in and destroyed Jerusalem and carried the people away captive.

After the exile, the city had to be restored; the walls and the temple were rebuilt. When Jesus, in the last days of His life, came to the temple, He turned to His disciples and said, "There will not be left here one stone upon another that will not be thrown down" (Matt. 24:2). God did it again. In AD 70, He ripped the city apart because the people had put their confidence in the institution; they had put their trust and their devotion in the religion rather than the living God. "And I will cast you out of my sight, as I cast out all your kinsmen, all the offspring of Ephraim" (Jer. 7:15). That is a hard saying indeed.

In every generation, people have put their confidence in their religious connections. The church is indeed a sacred institution; the visible church is not to be despised. Christ established His church, and the church is to be the body of our Lord Himself. But it is so easy for the church as an institution to become, instead of the body of Christ, a substitution for Christ. In that sense, the institution becomes antichrist insofar as it is a substitute that stands against the living Christ. Those who put their faith in the institution instead of Christ are trusting in a lie. The church cannot save you. The church did not die for you. The church cannot redeem you. The church did not purchase you. The church is not your savior. The church is the body of the Savior. It is the house of the Savior. We need to understand the difference.

12

When Bitter
Becomes Sweet

Ezekiel 2

The first chapter of Ezekiel has kept Old Testament scholars busy for centuries, with its vision of the whirlwind, strange creatures, and descriptions of strange conveyances with wheels within wheels that some have even tried to identify as flying saucers. We understand in the biblical imagery and literature that Ezekiel is having a vision of the transcendent majesty of God as He appears in His chariot throne, His movable throne, which is covered with glory and has the ability to shoot out in all different directions and appear here and there and everywhere, manifesting the appearance of God on His throne of judgment.

With that vision having been given in the first chapter, let's look and see what happens to Ezekiel in the second chapter. The first chapter ends with these words: "Such was the appearance of the likeness of the glory of the LORD. And when I saw it, I fell on my face, and I heard the voice of one speaking" (v. 28). Now, listen to what the voice says:

And he said to me, "Son of man, stand on your feet, and I will speak with you." And as he spoke to me, the Spirit entered into me and set me on my feet, and I heard him speaking to me. And he said to me, "Son of man, I send you to the people of Israel, to nations of rebels, who have rebelled against me. They and their fathers have transgressed against me to this very day. The descendants also are impudent and stubborn: I send you to them, and you shall say to them, 'Thus says the Lord God.' And whether they hear or refuse to hear (for they are a rebellious house) they will know that a prophet has been among them." (2:1–5)

This is a hard saying for Ezekiel. It's not easy to hear that people aren't going to listen to you, that they will hate your message. Therefore, God continues: "And you, son of man, be not afraid of them, nor be afraid of their words, though briers and thorns are with you and you sit on scorpions. Be not afraid of their words, nor be dismayed at their looks, for they are a rebellious house" (v. 6). Say that to a young minister who is about to be ordained and has to walk out on Sunday morning and stand before a congregation. Everybody who's ever spoken publicly knows what a contemptuous look looks like coming from the audience or from the congregation.

God goes on: "But you, son of man, hear what I say to you. Be not rebellious like that rebellious house; open your mouth and eat what I give you" (v. 8). Do you hear what God is saying? He's saying: "Ezekiel, I'm sending you to a rebellious people, and they are going to resist everything that you say. You will be speaking My word. They don't want My word. They've rebelled against My word. But that's not your responsibility. Understand, Ezekiel, that the people who will be angered by this word are actually angry at Me because it's My word. So don't worry about what they say and don't worry about what they do. You worry about Ezekiel. Don't you be rebellious. Don't you join in this host that resists My word." And then God says something incredible to Ezekiel: "'Open your mouth and eat what I give you.' And when I looked, behold, a hand was stretched out to me, and behold, a scroll of a book was in it. And he spread it before me. And it had writing on the front and on the back, and there were written on it words of lamentation and mourning and woe" (vv. 8–10).

Consider the hard saying that we have here. God says, "Eat what I give you," and Ezekiel looks and sees a hand stretched out, and in the hand is a scroll, which is written on in the front and on the back, on the inside and on the outside. The scroll is the word of God. It is a wonderful thing, a joyous thing, to announce peace to Jerusalem, to declare the gospel that people hear with great joy, to announce the good news of God's promise of mercy and forgiveness and redemption and love. That's not hard to do. But the scroll that God gives to Ezekiel does not contain this message. Instead, it contains lamentations, mourning, and woe. It's all bad news; it's all hard sayings.

The passage continues: "And he said to me, 'Son of man, eat whatever you find here. Eat this scroll, and go, speak to the house of Israel.' So I opened my mouth, and he gave me this scroll to eat. And he said to me, 'Son of man, feed your belly with this scroll that I give you and fill your stomach with it'" (3:1–3). Let's stop there for a moment. God says: "I'm not just going to put this word in your mouth and have you taste it and spit it out, nor am I asking you to chew on it for ten minutes and then discard it. I want you to put it in your mouth, to taste it, to chew it, to swallow it, and to digest it. I want it in your belly and then I want it in your bloodstream. I want it to be pervasive throughout your being. I want you to ingest it and I want you to digest it so that this word of Mine becomes a part of you." What word? Lamentations, woe, mourning, and grief are the word that God feeds His prophet.

Then something radical and astonishing takes place. Ezekiel says, "Then I ate it, and it was in my mouth as sweet as honey" (v. 3). How could this be? This scroll of laments, this scroll of mourning, this scroll of grief, this scroll of judgment, this scroll of the woes of God is taken by Ezekiel, and he eats it, expecting an unpalatable bitterness, something that will make him choke, something that will make him gasp, something that will make him retch. Instead, he tastes it, and it has the sweetness of honey.

You could look at that in different ways. You could say that Ezekiel is a sadistic prophet, someone who enjoys being the bearer of the judgment of God. He loves to go around and tell people how bad they are and how mad God is. But that wasn't the personality of Ezekiel or most of God's other prophets. They were men of compassion and immeasurable love, and yet God was able to make even His hard sayings taste as sweet as honey.

Jonathan Edwards struggled as a young theologian with the doctrine of God's sovereignty and election. He thought this doctrine indicated that God is arbitrary or capricious or unfair or cruel, but he kept trying to unravel this difficult and complex doctrine. Things came to him in stages, and Edwards said that in the first stage, he finally became convinced that the Scriptures really do teach a sovereign doctrine of election. Then he had an experience similar to that of Augustine centuries before. When he was reading from the New Testament, as he was reading the passage about the "immortal, invisible, the only wise God" (1 Tim. 1:17, KJV), the Spirit of God so illumined the text that Edwards had a glorious sense of the transcendent majesty of God, and suddenly he saw the whole concept of God's sovereignty and of His election in a totally different light. He said, "Now I was awakened to the sweetness of the doctrine."

I went through that same struggle. But now I see the message of God's gracious sovereign election as one of the sweetest messages in all Scripture. If we can get past all the problems that we have to struggle with intellectually with that doctrine and come to rest with the God who is sovereign, the hard saying that we initially recoil at is now as sweet as honey, and we are delighted to swallow it, to digest it, and to get it into our bloodstream.

We have a word in our language: *bittersweet*. It seems to be an oxymoron. How can something be both bitter and sweet at the same time? It can't be both bitter and sweet at the same time and in the same relationship. But even things that come to us initially clothed in bitterness can, under the agency of God's Holy Spirit, become sweet to us, and there is nothing sweeter to the Christian than God's Word. It is important for us, as we look at these difficult passages throughout Scripture, to look for the sweetness, to look for the beauty and the glory of God that stands behind them, for God's truth is always sweet. When we recoil against God's truth in a spirit of bitterness, it's because we haven't yet tasted to see that the Lord is good.

13

Behold the Day
of the Lord

Amos 5

Western culture retains a lingering influence from folklore, which includes a significant portion of fairy tales. Fairy tales are part of our heritage and have made their way into other media, from TV to literature to film. Many of these versions of fairy tales are upbeat and deliver a message of hope. They celebrate the victory of good over evil. There always seems to be the beautiful princess who is impoverished or suffering in some way, like Cinderella confined to the soot and the ashes of the hearth, who serendipitously has the opportunity, through the intervention of her fairy godmother, to go to the ball and meet the prince and live happily ever after.

In *Snow White and the Seven Dwarfs*, Snow White is yearning and dreaming of her future happiness and sings of her desire to meet her prince. She looks to the future for a day that would be her day of redemption, that would be her day of gladness; it would be the day when all her problems would be over. Have you ever done that? Have you ever looked forward to a particular date in your own chronology, apart from the return of Christ, looking for that hope of "when this happens, all my aspirations will be fulfilled"? Looking to the future in this way is common to human beings.

There is a concept in the Old Testament that is very important to the theology and the religion of Israel; it is called "the day of the Lord." If you trace that future promise early on in the life of the Jewish people throughout the Old Testament, you will see that the day of the Lord is a time of anticipated joy and pleasure and redemption. It is the day of God's visitation, the time when God will come and vindicate His people from all the persecution and suffering that they had received from wicked people and from wicked nations. It will be a time of unspeakable joy and celebration, when the majesty of God will become apparent and God Himself will appear in blazing glory and light, and all the nation will rejoice.

But as the history of Israel unfolds, the people grow more and more wicked and compromise the covenant more and more. They move further and further away from the law of God, and a storm cloud begins to develop that casts a shadow over this future promise of the day of the Lord. By the time we get to the eighth century BC, when God's wrath is now going to be poured out in judgment beginning with the northern kingdom of Israel in 722 and then later on, in the next century, moving to the destruction of Jerusalem in 586, the prophecies of the future become darker and darker.

We find one such prophecy in the words of the prophet Amos: "Therefore thus says the LORD, the God of hosts, the Lord: 'In all the squares there shall be wailing, and in all the streets they shall say, "Alas! Alas!" They shall call the farmers to mourning and to wailing those who are skilled in lamentation, and in all vineyards there shall be wailing, for I will pass through your midst,' says the LORD" (Amos 5:16–17). That is scary. This is not the promise of the Passover, when the angel of death passed over the houses of the Israelites. Now God is announcing that His angel is going to come not to Egypt but to Israel, not to pass over the land but to pass through it. When that happens, there will be weeping and wailing in the streets, and the people will be crying out, "Alas! Alas!"

The prophecy goes on: "Woe to you who desire the day of the LORD! Why would you have the day of the LORD? It is darkness, and not light, as if a man fled from a lion, and a bear met him, or went into the house and leaned his hand against the wall, and a serpent bit him. Is not the day of the LORD darkness, and not light, and gloom with no brightness in it?" (vv. 18–20). This is a dreadful statement. Think back for a moment to Cinderella standing at her windowsill, singing into the night and dreaming of her prince. Imagine that she discovers that the prince who comes is the prince of darkness, the prince of evil, the wicked prince who takes her away.

This is the kind of message that God is saying to His people: "You who long for the day of the Lord, you who are so caught up in the rapture of eschatological anticipation and hope, you can't wait today for the return of Jesus. You can't wait for the coming consummation of His kingdom. You read every forecast of His return. You watch every television program that announces the coming of Christ. You circle every passage in the New Testament that promises His glorious return on clouds of glory, when He will bring a new heaven and a new earth, and it causes you to rejoice in anticipation." That is their view of the day of the Lord. But Amos is speaking to a generation of people who desire the day of the Lord but who have become so estranged from God that the day of the Lord was not to be a good day for them. As Christians, we look forward to the return of Jesus with great anticipation, the day when our Prince will come and will set right all those things that are unjust in this world. We long for that day as a time of vindication, a time of healing for the nations, a time of the final realization of the fullness of our salvation. But what if our faith is a hypocritical faith? What if it's not real? What will happen to us on that day?

When the New Testament speaks of the return of Christ, it speaks of it in two different dimensions. On the one hand, it will be the day of final salvation for the people of God. On the other hand, it will be the day of final judgment when God's long-suffering and patience with wickedness will come to an end. So it will be a two-edged sword. For those who are saved, it will be the time of exquisite delight. For those who are not, it will be the ultimate time of judgment and doom.

What will it be for you? Will the time of Christ's appearing be a time when you will be enraptured with joy and blessedness to see the coming and manifestation of your Lord and of your Savior? Or will this be a moment of unspeakable horror when the Judge appears and calls you to account?

This is the warning that Amos gives: "You're looking for the day of the Lord, expecting a day of light. But I say to you, to those who are impenitent, that the day of the Lord will be a day of darkness." The greatest pleasure we can ever hope to enjoy is to experience the radiance of the countenance of Christ, the beholding of the manifestation of His unveiled glory. The Scriptures uniformly describe the majestic radiance of Christ in terms of light.

In the account of the book of Revelation of the new heaven and the new earth that comes down from heaven, it is said that there is no sun and there are no artificial means of illumination, because they're unnecessary. The light that is generated by the glory of God and by His Son will fill the holy city with light. Outside the new Jerusalem, we are told, will be a place of utter darkness where no light will shine, where the glory of God will not pierce and will not penetrate, and the radiance of the countenance of Christ will be shut out of this outer darkness. In the outer darkness there will be, as the Scriptures say, nothing but weeping and gnashing of teeth.

We were made for fellowship and communion with God. We were created with a capacity to experience unspeakable joy in His presence. To be shut out of that presence, to be in a place where there is no light and only darkness, is the worst possible thing that could ever befall us. From the lips of Amos we hear this dreadful announcement that the day of the Lord for some will be a day of darkness with no light in it.

This message is not pronounced out in the streets to pagans; it is pronounced to people who are professing the religion of the one true God. The prophecy goes on: "I hate, I despise your feasts, and I take no delight in your solemn assemblies. Even though you offer me your burnt offerings and grain offerings, I will not accept them; and the peace offerings of your fattened animals, I will not look upon them. Take away from me the noise of your songs; to the melody of your harps I will not listen. But let justice roll down like waters, and righteousness like an ever-flowing stream" (Amos 5:21–24). You see, God is talking to religious people. "I despise your feasts. I hate your solemn assemblies. The sacrifices that you've put on the altar have become a stench in My nostrils. Don't come into My presence with a show of religion while there's no righteousness in the land. You come with your sacrifices, but I won't accept them. You say your prayers, but I won't hear them. You sing your hymns, but I won't listen to them because the sound of your music has become sour in My ears." This should make us tremble.

God says, "The church is like a wadi in Israel," like a huge dry riverbed. There are two rainy seasons during the year in Israel. Most of the year, Israel is a desert, and those riverbeds are empty, with not a drop of water to be found within. When the rain does come, there is no place to contain the water, so all the water runs off the desert floor into these wadis, these big empty ditches, and then it becomes a raging torrent through the desert. God says: "That's what I want to see happen in My church. I want to see righteousness come rushing through the church and through the people of God like the flowing rivers in the empty wadis." But at that moment, God had looked at His people and found nothing but empty cisterns and empty riverbeds. They were empty of righteousness. These people professed faith but had no fruit, and for people like that, the day of the Lord will be a day of darkness with no light in it.

God announces a blessing to those who genuinely love the Lord's appearing. The promise of the future day of the Lord, for which we are still waiting, is a promise of blessedness. We call the coming of Christ the "blessed hope" of the church (Titus 2:13), and indeed it is the blessed hope of the church, and it is your blessed hope if you belong to Christ. I'm speaking now to people who are church members, who are churchgoers, who participate in the singing and in the prayers and in the sacraments and all the other aspects of worship. Is it real? Is your faith sincere? Does it inform your life? Is the fruit of righteousness flowing out of you? If it is, then the day of the Lord is a day of light for you, a day with no darkness in it.

14

Will a Man Rob God?

Malachi 3

It has been said on occasion in the church that the minister crosses the line and makes a transition from preaching to meddling. I'm afraid that this may be your feeling with this next hard saying because we are going to examine the question of tithing. I realize that I bring up this subject at the risk of meddling.

After my father died when I was a young man, my mother disposed of many of his personal effects but saved certain documents and items that had been important to them as a couple. A few years later when I became a Christian, my mother showed me some of these personal effects, and one was a handwritten sermon. My father was not a minister, but he was occasionally asked to speak in the Methodist church where he had grown up. Of all the things she could have saved, my mother had saved a copy of his handwritten sermon that he had preached. I was struck by its content and also by its title. The title of the sermon was simply "Will a Man Rob God?" It was a sermon on tithing. I remember that long before I was a Christian, just as a matter of family responsibility, it was instilled in my sister and me as young people that we had a duty and obligation to tithe. When we got our allowance as children, we were required to take a percentage of that allowance and put it into the collection plate on Sunday morning.

It wasn't until after I became a Christian that I discovered that this text was from the last book of the Old Testament, Malachi. We read in Malachi 3:8–10:

81

"Will man rob God? Yet you are robbing me. But you say, 'How have we robbed you?' In your tithes and contributions. You are cursed with a curse, for you are robbing me, the whole nation of you. Bring the full tithe into the storehouse, that there may be food in my house. And thereby put me to the test, says the LORD of hosts, if I will not open the windows of heaven for you and pour down for you a blessing until there is no more need.'"

This text raises many questions. First of all, is the principle of the tithe—that is, the command to give a tenth of one's increase to God, a principle that is clearly commanded by God in the Old Testament economy—one of the laws of God that carries over into the new covenant and imposes a like obligation on Christians? A second question arises: What is a tithe? The third question is this: To whom should the tithe be given? Finally, the fourth question, one that has been precipitated by the so-called health-and-wealth movement or prosperity gospel, is this: Does tithing guarantee a future prosperity for those who give it?

Is the principle of tithing given in the Old Testament something that carries over into the New Testament? To answer that question fully would require a series of lectures on the significance of the Old Testament law and to what degree it applies to the New Testament Christian. I'll simply say this: the New Testament does not explicitly restate this obligation. The New Testament is a little bit more ambiguous. If anything, however, the New Testament imposes a greater obligation on the people of God in light of the clear teaching in the new covenant that we live in a better covenant, that we have more blessings bestowed on us than the people of the Old Testament did, that the riches we receive from God in the New Testament are greater than those that abounded in the Old Testament. So from a simple process of reasoning, it would seem that as the benefits increase, so the responsibilities increase proportionately, even as God Himself says in the New Testament, "Everyone to whom much was given, of him much will be required" (Luke 12:48). We are also told in the New Testament that we are to give as the Lord prospers us. So the principle of giving to the work of God is certainly reaffirmed in the New Testament.

Then we must understand what the guidelines are for the principle of supporting the work of God in the New Testament. To do so, let's look at the second question: What is a tithe? The word *tithe* means "a tenth." The way it worked in Israel was this: God had separated one tribe, the Levites, from the family of Jacob to be responsible for ministering in the tabernacle and temple and the matters of the religious community, and they were not to have to look for secular employment to meet their needs. The other tribes were responsible to support the Levites' work by the giving of the tithe. The purpose of the tithe was to underwrite the work of God in the midst of the people. Two things are often overlooked. The Levites were responsible not only for the ministry of the tabernacle and the temple but also for the religious instruction of the nation. They were both the ministers and the teachers. Correspondingly, there are seminaries and Christian colleges today that also often receive some of the funding provided for the work of God.

In an agrarian society, people were either farmers or ranchers. Suppose that you had a herd of five hundred cows and that during the course of the year this herd produced ten calves (let's just use that number for the sake of simplicity). If the cattle rancher in Israel had to give 10 percent of his increase to the Lord, he would have to present one of those calves to the Levites as the payment of his tithe. It was not 10 percent of the total worth of his herd, which in the case of a herd of five hundred cows and ten new calves would mean giving fifty-one cows. Likewise, those who grew produce had to give 10 percent of the increase of their produce back to the Lord. The thing that is so striking about the Old Testament principle of the tithe or the tenth is its equity; every person in the land was required to tithe, to give 10 percent of his increase to the work of God. There was no progressive income tax in Israel.

A progressive income tax would have been viewed by God and by the Jewish nation as an injustice. In such a system, those with greater increase pay a higher percentage of taxes, which tends to make economics become politicized. In Israel, everyone had to pay the same percentage, not the same amount, so the wealthy person had to give a lot more produce or a lot more of his wealth to the work of the kingdom than the poor person. This system also avoided the lionizing of the wealthy for their giving, for the wealthy were simply doing their duty and were expressing their gratitude for this prosperity that they had enjoyed. In our culture, we tend to fawn over the big givers, even if the big givers are giving less than 10 percent. Under the economy of the tithe, someone who gave less than 10 percent was a thief in God's eyes no matter how much he gave because he was robbing God of what he was actually required to give.

A survey once revealed that of those Americans who identify as evangelical Christians, only 4 percent say that they tithe. If that's the case, then 96 percent of professing Christians in the United States are consistently, systematically stealing from God. This is a serious problem. Churches and godly ministries that are striving to make an impact in this world often struggle with insufficient resources, and the reason is that they are working on only 4 percent of what they should have to fulfill their mission. God regarded this matter as serious enough that He would curse His people if they withheld their tithes and offerings from Him.

To whom was the tithe given? In the Old Testament, the tithe was taken into the storehouse, a central depository that received the produce, the animals, and so on. The Levites would then allocate and dispense the resources to those who were in the Levitical system. Some ministers today say that the tithe must be paid to the local church alone because only the church represents the storehouse. It is then the responsibility of the church to distribute those tithes and offerings to various ministries and so on. To be consistent with this view, we would have to advocate that all the tithes be given to a central agency within the denomination and then allocated to the individual churches. Most of those who hold to this view would not be on board with such a practice.

It seems to me that one of the requirements of membership in a local church should be the vow to support the ministry of that church with your offerings and with your tithes. A Christian ought to give the majority of his tithe to his local church, but I don't think he's required to give it all there.

This passage ends with a promise from God: "And thereby put me to the test, says the Lord of hosts, if I will not open the windows of heaven for you and pour down for you a blessing until there is no more need" (Mal. 3:10). This promise of blessing is one of the most abused texts you will ever see today. Appeal letters sometimes promise that if you will send a ministry a donation of $50, God will return $500 or $5,000 to you based on God's promise that He will open up the window of blessing. That is a way to manipulate people to sacrificial giving, which is abhorrent. This is an abuse of a real promise of God.

Sometimes people claim that they cannot afford to tithe. What they actually mean is that they cannot afford their current lifestyle while also tithing. That's why it's so important that we start tithing early so that we become accustomed to it.

Then people argue about whether you should tithe on your gross or your net. My practice has been to see my first obligation as giving 10 percent to God. It's not my money. I can't afford to steal from God. If I hold it back, I'm embezzling from my Creator and my Redeemer. I have to give what is my responsibility. The freeing thing is that if I'm prosperous and I've done what I'm supposed to do, I'm free to enjoy the fruit of my labor as long as I'm a good steward and prudent with it. I have never missed a single penny that I have tithed because God indeed provides for us in such a way that one of the best investments we can make in this world is in the kingdom of God.

15

The Unpardonable Sin

Matthew 12

One of the most difficult passages in all the New Testament, a passage that certainly qualifies for the category of *hard sayings*, is where Jesus speaks about an unforgivable sin, the sin of blasphemy against the Holy Spirit. Let's take a look at Matthew's account of it: "Therefore I tell you, every sin and blasphemy will be forgiven people, but the blasphemy against the Spirit will not be forgiven. And whoever speaks a word against the Son of Man will be forgiven, but whoever speaks against the Holy Spirit will not be forgiven, either in this age or in the age to come" (12:31–32).

It's obvious why this passage has become such a problem to so many people. It describes and discusses a sin that is unforgivable. Many people wonder whether they have committed that sin. They labor painfully under the fear that they have in fact sinned in such a way that it has excluded them from any possibility of forgiveness, either here or at the judgment seat of Christ. There are Christians who live in mortal fear that they might at some point commit that sin that would cause them to lose their salvation and to lose the hope of heaven.

Our Lord is teaching something that is hard. He clearly states that there is a sin that is unforgivable, and He clearly identifies that unforgivable sin as "blasphemy against the [Holy] Spirit." We don't have to wrestle with ambiguity in that regard. But as soon as we ask the next question, we plunge into a sea of ambiguity and of great difficulty. The question is this: What is this unforgivable sin that Jesus identifies as blasphemy against the Holy Spirit?

There have been many attempts in church history to answer this question. Some have identified it with murder because murderers are to be put to death. Others have identified it with adultery because the body is the temple of the Holy Spirit, and to commit adultery, Paul tells us, is to sin against Him. We have an immediate problem with these options, though. David was guilty of murder, and he was able to receive forgiveness. He was also guilty of adultery and likewise was able to receive forgiveness. Therefore, we must rule those two theories out.

Jesus is talking about blasphemy, something that is done verbally, either in writing or through the spoken word. Even someone as brilliant as Augustine argued that the unforgivable sin is total and final unbelief—that is, if a person persists to the end of his life in rejecting Christ, he will not receive a second chance in heaven. Such unbelief is ultimately and permanently unforgivable. Augustine was right about the results of permanent unbelief, for there is no reason to hope for a second chance after the grave. If you have rejected Him up to a certain point in your life, however, even if it's very late in life, you may still be forgiven if you turn and trust in Him.

Jesus in this passage makes a distinction between a sin committed against Him and a sin committed against the Holy Spirit. I think that's what makes the problem all the more difficult. Let's look again at verse 32: "And whoever speaks a word against the Son of Man will be forgiven, but whoever speaks against the Holy Spirit will not be forgiven, either in this age or in the age to come." This suggests that one can blaspheme Christ or blaspheme the Father, and that as long as you don't blaspheme the Holy Spirit, you still have an opportunity to be forgiven. You can feel the weight of that difficulty. What difference does it make whether we blaspheme the Father, the Son, or the Holy Spirit? Surely it's just as heinous to blaspheme against the Father or against the Son as it is to blaspheme against the Holy Spirit.

Blasphemy is something that we say that denigrates the character of God. If every form of blasphemy against God were unforgivable, none of us would have a prayer because we have all blasphemed. If every sin against the Holy Spirit were unforgivable, we would not have a chance because all of us at some point have grieved the Holy Spirit in one way or another.

This is what makes this passage excruciatingly difficult. The Bible seems to give us provision for forgiveness of all kinds of blasphemies, but there is one particular kind of blasphemy that is unforgivable. Jesus particularly applies this blasphemy to the Holy Spirit when He says that a word against the Son of Man, obviously referring to Himself, is forgivable. Not only does Jesus preach that it is forgivable, but He practices what He preaches when He's on the cross as the Son of Man, as the Lord of glory, in the midst of His own crucifixion. When people are mocking Him and ridiculing Him and blaspheming Him, He utters a prayer for those people by saying to the Father, "Father, forgive them." Why? "Father, forgive them, for *they know not what they do*" (Luke 23:34, emphasis added). This doesn't mean that they were excused; just because they were ignorant of what they were doing does not automatically excuse them.

In the Old Testament sacrificial system, special provisions were given for sins done in ignorance. This is part of the reason, incidentally, that the Roman Catholic Church has historically made an important distinction in its moral theology between two kinds of ignorance: *vincible ignorance* and *invincible ignorance*. Something that is *invincible* is unbeatable; you can't conquer it and you can't defeat it. Something that is *vincible* can be conquered, can be overcome; it is something that can be beaten. What does Rome mean when it gives us this distinction between vincible and invincible ignorance? Let me explain with an illustration.

I live in the state of Florida. Suppose I drive my car into the state of Georgia, and I enter a little village there, and I come to an intersection where there's a traffic light. The traffic light is red, but I don't want to stop for the light, and I just go through the red light. The next thing I see is another red light, only this time it's on the roof of a car behind me. It's flashing, and here come the police. They pull me over and say, "Did you see that red light back there?" I reply, "Yes, I did." "Well, then, why didn't you stop?" "I didn't know you were supposed to stop. I plead ignorance. I had no idea that I was supposed to stop." The officer says, "Let me see your driver's license." I show him my driver's license. He asks, "Don't you have red traffic lights in Florida?" "Yes." "What do you have to do there?" "Well, sir, in Florida I know I'm supposed to stop at a red light at an intersection, and I stop at red lights in Florida. But I'm not in Florida now; I'm driving here in Georgia. How was I supposed to know that Georgia law requires me to stop at a red light?" Think about that. How far do you think that argument would go before the magistrate if I tried to dodge the ticket by pleading ignorance? It's tacitly understood that if I presume to drive my car in any state of this union, I assume responsibility to know what the traffic laws and the motor vehicle regulations are in that state, and I am held accountable. Why? Those laws are published, they're public, they're easily accessible, and I am responsible to know what the rules are before I drive my car in that state. Even if I didn't know that the traffic light meant "stop" in Georgia, I had the opportunity to know it, my ignorance could have been easily overcome, and I can't plead ignorance as an excuse.

We do lots of things out of ignorance. We disobey God out of ignorance in lots of ways, and we're going to plead ignorance on the final day. Those arguments are not going to work because the Word has been given to us and we should know what the Word of God is. Sometimes we sin in ignorance. We sin in ignorance because we have neglected a sober, diligent study of the things of God, things that God has made perfectly clear and readily accessible to us. We must be careful of trying to hide behind the cloak of ignorance as an excuse.

Yet there is such a thing as invincible ignorance, as the Roman Catholic Church teaches. Now let's change the scenario. Suppose that the city fathers of Orlando are facing a budget squeeze and need to raise money in a hurry, so the city council gets together this evening and concludes: "Tomorrow morning at seven o'clock, we're going to have a new law in the city that everybody who drives into the city has to stop on green and go on red. If you drive through a green light, it's going to be a $100 fine. We'll post police at every traffic intersection, and we'll make a fortune because we're not going to tell anybody that we've changed the law." The next morning, we drive into the city. We see a green light; we go through the green light. The next thing you know, we're pulled over and we're arrested for driving through this green light. If we plead ignorance before the magistrate, do we have a just defense? Yes, of course we do, because that ignorance was invincible. There was no possible way we could have known that the rules had been changed in the middle of the game.

The ignorance that the people had when they brought Jesus to the cross and crucified Him did not excuse them. They were guilty of crucifying Christ, and they should have known better. Had they searched the Scriptures, they would have seen that Jesus fulfilled the Scriptures and was not the villain that they declared Him to be. Even though their ignorance was vincible ignorance and not invincible ignorance, Jesus interceded for them on the cross, saying, "Father, forgive them; they don't know what they're doing." You see the same kind of thing when the Apostles are rehearsing to the Jewish community the travesty of the crucifixion of Christ. Paul states, "For if they had [understood], they would not have crucified the Lord of glory" (1 Cor. 2:8). A certain forbearance is given in the Scriptures to those who were responsible for the death of Christ, an acknowledgment of a certain level of ignorance.

For us to understand the passage in Matthew 12, I think it's critical that we look at what precedes this warning that Jesus gives. If we go back to verses 22–24, we read this account: "Then a demon-oppressed man who was blind and mute was brought to him, and he healed him, so that the man spoke and saw. And all the people were amazed, and said, 'Can this be the Son of David?' But when the Pharisees heard it, they said, 'It is only by Beelzebul, the prince of demons, that this man casts out demons.'" People recognized in the miracles of Christ the manifestation of the Messiah, the Son of David. But the archenemies of Jesus wouldn't acknowledge His identity even then, and they accused Jesus of performing His works by the power of Satan. That is blasphemy. It is blasphemy to accuse Jesus Christ of being satanic, of being in league with the devil.

It's on this occasion that Jesus, knowing their thoughts, according to the gospel, takes the opportunity to give this very severe warning to the Pharisees. It's as if Jesus is saying: "You've been plotting and conspiring, and you haven't listened to Me. You have rejected Me. You've done all these things, and I've patiently taken it, but you are coming now to a line in the sand, and if you cross that line, you're going to forfeit any possibility of forgiveness either now or in the future." He couches that in terms of this distinction between speaking against Him and speaking against the Holy Spirit.

Hebrews 6 and 10 indicate a falling away of the distinction between blaspheming against Christ and blaspheming against the Holy Spirit once a person has been illuminated and has received from the Holy Spirit the clear revelation that Jesus is the Christ. If the Holy Spirit has opened your eyes and caused you to see that Jesus is the Christ, and then, after knowing by the power of the Holy Spirit that Jesus is the Son of God, you accuse Jesus of being satanic, you have now committed the unforgivable sin.

On the one hand, the only kind of person who could theoretically commit the blasphemy against the Holy Spirit would be a Christian because Christians are the only people who have received this revelation and have a clear understanding, by virtue of the power of the Holy Spirit, that Jesus is the Son of God. They're the only ones who know full well that Jesus is not satanic. That's the bad news. The good news is that it is theoretical. All of us are capable of that kind of sin and evil, but none of us has committed or will commit that sin because this is the very thing for which Jesus intercedes on our behalf at the throne of grace, that we will be preserved from falling and from losing the salvation that He has purchased for us. Though the warning to the Pharisees is a real warning, this is not something that needs to concern us in terms of the possibility of losing our salvation. It's not that we shouldn't be concerned about our speech and our actions and so on, but no one who is in Christ, who has been made alive by the Holy Spirit, who has known the illumination of His knowledge of the identity of Christ, would ever sink so far as to accuse Jesus of being satanic.

It's not that we're incapable of committing such a heinous sin in and of ourselves, but our Lord is gracious enough to hold our tongues from it and to preserve us from this ghastly crime. There is still a call to be vigilant, however. One of the Ten Commandments demands the safeguarding of the sanctity of the name of God. Christians need to be exceedingly careful with their tongues—about how they speak of Christ, how they speak of God, and how they speak of the Holy Spirit. It is extremely offensive to God to have His name used in vain, and I doubt that anything is more offensive to the Father than to hear the name of His beloved Son used as a common, ordinary curse word.

For those of you who are not believers, using the name of Christ frequently and casually may be part of your practice. I plead with you to think about what you're doing, that you are heaping abuse on the One whom God has appointed to be your Judge and our Redeemer.

16

Image Is
Not Everything

Mark 11

You will recall that by *hard sayings* we mean those passages in Scripture that could be hard in one of two ways: either because the message comes across as somewhat harsh and difficult to accept or because it is puzzling and difficult for us to understand. We're going to look at a passage that fits into the second category. It's found in more than one place in Scripture, but we'll look at the version in Mark's gospel. It is the story of Jesus' cursing the fig tree: "On the following day, when they came from Bethany, he was hungry. And seeing in the distance a fig tree in leaf, he went to see if he could find anything on it. When he came to it, he found nothing but leaves, for it was not the season for figs. And he said to it, 'May no one ever eat fruit from you again.' And his disciples heard it" (Mark 11:12–14).

Several matters come into view when approaching this text. Some people have said that in this episode, Jesus reveals a side to His character that is somewhat dark. Some have even gone so far as to say that on this occasion Jesus sins and disqualifies Himself from the role of sinless Savior because He behaves in a manner that is capricious and arbitrary, and He has an outburst against this poor, innocent tree simply because it doesn't have any figs. People have such consternation about this because of the phrase that Mark inserts in the text: that "it was not the season for figs." Jesus, after all, knew that it wasn't the season for figs, so why should He curse a fig tree for not bearing figs when it wasn't even the season for figs?

In Palestine, there is a definite season for figs, but there are several different varieties or species of fig trees. One particular variety bears figs at a different time of the year from all the other varieties of fig trees. This particular tree is coveted in the Near East because it provides this delicacy out of season. When one would stumble upon that particular variety of fig tree outside fig season, it would be a particular delight because the fruit of the tree could then be enjoyed. When that particular variety of fig tree had leaves on it, that was a sure sign of the presence of figs. The absolute principle by which one determined whether figs were available was not what season it was but whether the fig tree had leaves on it.

Imagine the scene. Jesus and His disciples are walking, they're hungry, and Jesus notices in the distance this particular variety of fig tree, and obviously He could see that it had leaves, which meant to Jesus and to the disciples that they could enjoy a serendipitous treat of out-of-season figs. As Jesus draws near to the tree, lo and behold, there are all these leaves but no figs, so Jesus curses the fig tree. The reason that He curses the fig tree is twofold. In the first instance, the tree was supposed to have figs and it didn't. It had all the outward signs of bearing figs, but it had no fruit. It's not as if a fig tree is a moral agent that can be guilty of the sin of hypocrisy; trees are not hypocritical because they don't make conscious decisions to lie or deceive or defraud and playact the way hypocrites do. But second, Jesus takes advantage of this situation from the realm of nature to make a point, to teach a lesson. The kind of lesson being taught here is what we call an object lesson.

There is a grand tradition among the prophets of the Old Testament not only to speak their messages but at times to dramatize them by the use of external objects or external signs. Isaiah went through the city naked on one occasion to dramatize a point that God was trying to communicate to His people. The prophets would frequently use such object lessons to illustrate the divine message, and that's what Jesus is doing here. Jesus is demonstrating a truth of God by using the fig tree as an object lesson, and if we look further in the text, we will see that.

After verse 14, as a sort of interruption in the episode, we have the account of Jesus' cleansing the temple in Jerusalem. In verse 20, Mark comes back to the business of the fig tree:

As they passed by in the morning [this is the following day], they saw the fig tree withered away to its roots. And Peter remembered and said to him, "Rabbi, look! The fig tree that you cursed has withered." And Jesus answered them, "Have faith in God. Truly, I say to you, whoever says to this mountain, 'Be taken up and thrown into the sea,' and does not doubt in his heart, but believes that what he says will come to pass, it will be done for him. Therefore I tell you, whatever you ask in prayer, believe that you have received it, and it will be yours." (vv. 20–24)

This explanation in a sense muddies the waters because it's obvious that the point that Jesus is making is about hypocrisy. The fig tree manifested something that was not true. We can glean from this incident, without further elucidation, the point that Jesus made consistently with the Pharisees about hypocrisy. Jesus consistently criticized the Pharisees for their externalism— that is, their tremendous outward show of piety and of righteousness. They paraded their piety before men, and Jesus said that they were like whitewashed tombs that were gleaming on the outside, but inside were dead men's bones. Jesus frequently makes this criticism of the Pharisees, whom He addresses as hypocrites for displaying one thing on the surface that was not a true manifestation of what was really there inside.

You can see the analogy between that and the fig tree that displayed the presence of leaves, but there was no fruit in the tree. That exonerates Jesus from any charge of irrational anger. Jesus frequently illustrates from nature the spiritual truths that He wants to say. He says that a tree that does not bring forth fruit is worthy to be cut down and cast into the fire, and then He turns around and uses that to illustrate the necessity of the Christian to bear fruit in the Christian life and that those who do not bear fruit will be cut down and cast aside. This is again illustrated by His cursing of the fig tree.

The thing that is so often missed in this incident is the remarkable fact of what actually happened. Our Lord manifests His humanity in several dimensions here. One indicates that the reason He went to the fig tree in the first place was that He was hungry. We also observe that He didn't know in advance that the tree would not have figs, so according to His human nature, He was not omniscient. Yet when He wants to demonstrate the message of the object lesson, He calls on His supernatural power to wither the tree on command.

This is one more incident in the life of Jesus when Jesus demonstrates His power over nature. It's not dissimilar from the occasion on the Sea of Galilee when He caused the storm to cease and the waters to become calm. He said to the sea that was raging, "Peace! Be still!" (Mark 4:39), and instantly the sea was calm. In like manner, He now addresses another part of nature, and by the sheer power of His command, He causes that tree to die.

The emphasis of this episode is the lesson that God is not interested in our giving outward signs of producing fruit, but He wants to see real fruit in our lives. It's not enough simply to go through the motions of prayer and of Bible study and of church attendance and even of preaching and teaching. God wants to see the fruit of His grace, the fruit of the Holy Spirit, being brought forth in abundance in our lives because there is a sweetness to the fruit of the Spirit, a sweetness that can be enjoyed by all who are hungry and by all who are mourning and by all who are troubled. Sometimes in our nation we get overly concerned about productivity, and sometimes we disclaim the Protestant work ethic. But Jesus frequently exhorted His followers to be productive, to bring forth the fruit of the labors of the kingdom of God, and that's our lesson from this episode.

17

Why Didn't Jesus Know?

Mark 13

There is another hard saying that, like the passage in Mark 11, concerns fig trees in a way. It's found just two chapters later, and it is another of the kind of hard saying that is puzzling and difficult to understand. As a result, it has provoked no small amount of controversy throughout the history of the church. In Mark 13:26–27 we read: "And then they will see the Son of Man coming in clouds with great power and glory. And then he will send out the angels and gather his elect from the four winds, from the ends of the earth to the ends of heaven."

After this, Jesus immediately gives a little parable called the parable of the fig tree. He says this: "From the fig tree learn its lesson: as soon as its branch becomes tender and puts out its leaves, you know that summer is near. So also, when you see these things taking place, you know that he is near, at the very gates. Truly, I say to you, this generation will not pass away until all these things take place" (vv. 28–30). He goes on to say, "Heaven and earth will pass away, but my words will not pass away" (v. 31).

Now here comes the hard saying. Jesus says in verses 32–33: "But concerning that day or that hour, no one knows, not even the angels in heaven, nor the Son, but only the Father. Be on guard, keep awake. For you do not know when the time will come."

Some people look at the Bible and see it as a kind of code. They figure out which character or event in the Bible corresponds to which person or event in history, they unravel all the metaphors, and they lay out the dates in such a way that they claim to be able to know when Jesus is coming back. They name the year, the month, and even sometimes the day. Some people will not even be discouraged by failed predictions but will say that their next prediction will surely be right.

It seems strange that such people take it upon themselves to claim to know something that Jesus Himself didn't know—that is, the day and the hour of His return. It seems that every year somebody gets out a calculator, gets out a Bible, and speculates on the day and the hour in spite of the very plain and clear statement of our Lord that even He didn't know the day and the hour, and furthermore that this day and hour is known by no man.

What is the hard part of this saying? Jesus says, "But concerning that day or that hour, no one knows, not even the angels in heaven, nor the Son, but only the Father" (v. 32). We speak of the Trinity as Father, Son, and Holy Spirit, and we affirm with the Westminster Confession of Faith that all the members of the Trinity are God and all participate in the attributes of God. The Father is eternal, the Son is eternal, and the Holy Spirit is eternal. The Father is immutable, the Son is immutable, and the Holy Spirit is immutable. The Father is omnipresent, the Son is omnipresent, and the Holy Spirit is omnipresent. What else do we ascribe to all three persons of the Godhead? We ascribe the attribute of omniscience, meaning "all knowledge." Here it seems that Jesus is saying that there is some information, some knowledge, that only the Father has and that the Son doesn't have it, the angels don't have it, and presumably the Holy Spirit doesn't have it either. Are we saying that there is an attribute that only one member of the Godhead possesses while the others do not have it? To put it in the simplest terms possible, how could Jesus be God incarnate and have this gap in His knowledge? How is it possible that Jesus could not know the day and the hour of His own return?

Many interesting theories have been set forth about this, not the least of which comes from the mind of Thomas Aquinas. I'm going to give you a shorthand version of Thomas' theory on this. Thomas was deeply troubled by this statement, and he said in effect: "Wait a minute. Jesus is the God-man. Jesus has two natures—a human nature and a divine nature—and those two natures are perfectly united and joined together. How is it possible that the God-man could not know something?"

In the first instance, we have to ask, Who is the "Son" that Jesus is referring to? When the "Son" is mentioned, obviously that refers to Jesus, but sometimes we use this term "Son" strictly with reference to the divine person in the Godhead—Father, Son, and Holy Spirit. The Son of God existed before the incarnation. There is the eternal Son, the second person of the Trinity, who assumed a human nature at the incarnation. Sometimes we use the phrase "Son of God" to refer to the incarnate Son of God; in other words, we use it to refer to Jesus. When Jesus says that not even the Son knows, but only the Father knows, is He speaking in strict Trinitarian terms about the eternal Godhead, or is He speaking of Himself in His incarnation, wherein He had taken on human flesh? I suspect Jesus is speaking in the second sense. I don't think for a minute that the eternal Son of God has a gap in His knowledge. If He does, then we have to abandon the doctrine of the Trinity. The text does not demand that we attribute this lack of knowledge to the eternal Son, however; instead, it demands that we attribute it to the incarnate Son. The incarnate Son not only has a divine nature but also has a human nature, and omniscience is not an attribute of human beings, not even Jesus in His incarnation. According to His human nature, Jesus is not omniscient.

This is the struggle that Thomas Aquinas had. He said that even if Jesus does not know everything according to His human nature, there is such a perfect union between the human and divine natures that anything that Jesus knows according to His divine nature He must also know according to His human nature. That was Thomas' thinking. He came up with the *theory of accommodation*, which states that Jesus did know the day and the hour, but it was sacred information. It was holy information. It was information that was not the will of God to reveal to mortal people. Jesus, in order to accommodate Himself to the weakness of His hearers, simply told them that He didn't know because it wasn't for them to know. The knowledge was too high, too holy, too wonderful to be communicated. But He actually did know.

That theory of Thomas was later incorporated in a papal encyclical and became the official position of the Roman Catholic Church, buttressed by a concept called the *communication of attributes*. That is the view that in the union between the divine and human natures, certain attributes from the divine nature are communicated to or shared with the human nature. Omniscience, for example, is communicated to the human nature from the divine nature. This became even more controversial in questions about the Lord's Supper because the Roman Catholic Church believes in the doctrine of transubstantiation, meaning that in the miracle of the Mass, at the time of consecration, the elements of the bread and wine are transformed into the actual body and blood of Christ.

The question becomes this: If the Mass is being celebrated all around the world, often at the same time, how is it possible for Jesus' body and blood to be in all these different places at once if body and blood, as properties of the human nature, are confined to one place? Obviously, the physical flesh of Jesus does not belong to His divine nature; it belongs to His human nature. For part of His human nature to be present at more than one place at the same time would require omnipresence. But omnipresence is not an attribute of humanity; it is an attribute of deity. The Roman Catholic Church said it is possible because in the perfect unity between the divine nature and the human nature, the power of omnipresence is communicated from the divine nature to the human nature. That was the idea held by Thomas Aquinas (and in a modified form by Martin Luther, I should add).

This creates a problem in theology. At the ecumenical church council at Chalcedon in the fifth century, the dual nature of Christ was definitively defined as *vera homo, vera Deus*—that is, "truly human, truly divine." The council also used four negatives to describe the relations between the human and divine natures of Christ, saying that the two natures in this mysterious union are without confusion, mixture, separation, or division. That is to say, in the incarnation, the divine nature did not become humanized nor the human nature deified. The natures weren't blended or mixed together, but they were joined; they were united without being confused. Finally, the council stated that "each nature retain[s] its own attributes." This means that in the incarnation, the divine nature stays divine. It still has omniscience; it still has omnipotence; it still has eternality. The human nature, when it is joined with that divine nature, is still considered the human nature; though you can't divide it or separate it from the divine nature, you can distinguish it and must distinguish it from the divine nature, but the human nature remains human. It has a physical aspect that the divine nature does not. It's mutable; it undergoes changes and is not immutable like the divine nature. We see Jesus grow up. We see Him learn. We see Him experience pain. We see all the manifestations of the human nature, yet without sin.

How, then, do we deal with this passage in Mark 13? Why don't we take Jesus at His word? Thomas Aquinas bends over backward to find a way for Jesus to remain omniscient. If ever there was a case when Homer nodded, when the genius took a nap, I think it was here. Even the great Thomas Aquinas flubbed this one, because what he does is to keep his concept of the incarnation intact, but at a very serious cost. He has Jesus telling His disciples something that is not true. Thomas can try to give us all kinds of justifying reasons of accommodation, but Jesus is flatly saying, "I don't know the day or the hour of My return." Now, if He does know and tells His disciples that He doesn't know, that's a lie. If it's a lie, no matter how small, that's all it would take to destroy His sinlessness and disqualify Him as the Savior. I would much prefer to say, "Jesus said He didn't know, so He didn't know."

Obviously, according to His divine nature, Jesus knew, but He is speaking now according to His human nature. Sometimes, Jesus speaks according to His divine nature, as when He said that He saw Nathanael before He ever met him. He knew what other people were thinking. Jesus had supernatural knowledge at His disposal, but the divine nature obviously didn't communicate everything it knew to the human nature. So when Jesus says, "I don't know the day or the hour," He's merely expressing to us that according to His human nature, He is limited in His knowledge. Even then, however, He always speaks the truth.

This is not to divide the two natures; it's to distinguish them. When Jesus bleeds, does He bleed divine blood? No, blood is a property of humanity. Hunger is something that happens to human beings, not to God. Sweat is a human property, not a divine property. A limitation of knowledge is a manifestation of human nature, not of divine nature. So we must distinguish at this point and say that what Jesus said is true. He meant what He said, that according to His human nature He did not know the day or the hour of His own return.

You may wonder why it matters whether Jesus was omniscient or not omniscient in His human nature and His divine nature. Let me suggest that the further we delve into the Scriptures and into the things of God, the deeper and more complex these things become. But even though we may wrestle with it at a somewhat technical theological level, that does not mean that there are no practical consequences of this. As Christians, we want to understand as much as we possibly can about the person of Christ. He is our Lord, and yet if we have the deepest theological knowledge available to us as human beings, we still run head-on into a mystery when it comes to the incarnation. Who can fathom the depths of this union between God and man? But one of the things that the church has done for us over the centuries, such as at the Council of Nicaea and later at the Council of Chalcedon, is to draw lines in the sand. The church has put boundaries or borders around us, showing us that we can speculate, but that there are limits to our speculations. There are lines that we cannot cross or we will end up in serious heresy.

18

When Towers Fall

Luke 13

In April 1995, a man named Timothy McVeigh detonated a bomb beneath a federal office building in Oklahoma City. At least 168 people were killed in the explosion and nearly seven hundred were injured, including more than a dozen children at a day-care facility in the building. The nation watched the news reports in horror. It was one of those rare occasions when the news media, rushing to bring fresh information to the viewers, brought in unedited tapes, and our usual shield from gory reports of violence in the world was absent. A memorable image from the rescue and recovery effort showed a firefighter cradling a deceased infant in his arms. The aftermath was so horrific that reporters and anchors groped in vain for ways to adequately describe the heinousness of this crime. I heard one newsman say that this was an inhuman, satanic act, and another newsman said: "Wait a minute. We have to realize that people are capable of this kind of atrocity."

There was a national sense of outrage, particularly because children were killed and injured as well. Many people asked an age-old question as a result: Why? Why would someone do this? And perhaps more pointedly, Why would God allow this? The question comes up again and again as we witness disasters and atrocities in our world, from natural catastrophes to school shootings to acts of terrorism.

We see a similar drama play out in the gospel of Luke:

There were some present at that very time who told him about the Galileans whose blood Pilate had mingled with their sacrifices. And he answered
them, "Do you think that these Galileans were worse sinners than all the
other Galileans, because they suffered in this way? No, I tell you; but unless
you repent, you will all likewise perish. Or those eighteen on whom the
tower in Siloam fell and killed them: do you think that they were worse
offenders than all the others who lived in Jerusalem? No, I tell you; but
unless you repent, you will all likewise perish." (13:1–5)

The questions that were being brought to Jesus were about catastrophes that had befallen people in their day. They were wondering how a good
God, a loving God, could allow these tragic catastrophes to take place. It's
hard enough to understand how human beings could be so inhumane and so
wicked in their treatment of other human beings, but how could God allow
these things to happen? Every generation seeks to answer those questions, and
the people in Jesus' day were no different.

The people reported to Jesus two specific incidents that they found trou-
bling. The first one was an event that took place in Galilee while people were
in the midst of worship. Some of the soldiers under the authority of Pontius
Pilate came in and massacred them, mixing their blood with the blood of some
animals. These were not warriors on the battlefield who were killed; they were
supplicants in a worship environment. The people asked Jesus, "How can this
be?" Jesus answered, "Do you think that these Galileans were worse sinners
than all the other Galileans, because they suffered in this way?" (v. 2). Jesus, in
a sense, avoids their question and takes this opportunity to instruct them on a
very weighty and difficult theological truth.

Jesus answers the question with a question, and it's very similar to the
response He gave elsewhere in His ministry as recorded in the gospel of John.
People brought a man who had been blind from birth to Jesus and asked this
question, trying to trap Jesus with a theological conundrum: "Who sinned,
this man or his parents, that he was born blind?" (John 9:2). Those who raised
that question committed an informal fallacy of logic called the *fallacy of the
false dilemma*, sometimes called the *either/or fallacy*. They came to Jesus and
gave Him only two options to account for the man's blindness. "Either the
man was born blind because of his own sin or he was born blind because of the

sin of his parents." How does Jesus answer that question? "Neither." It didn't have anything to do with this man's sin or his parents' sin, but it happened that God might be glorified. He was, indeed, glorified through the healing of the man born blind. Behind that question was the assumption that all suffering in this world is proportionately related to a person's particular degree of sinfulness. This is a weighty matter.

Many people struggle with a nagging sense that their suffering is a result of their sin, that they have done something wrong at some point that has led them to the awful situation that they are in now. We hardly ever talk about this because we want to divorce ourselves from any thought that there is a relationship between sin and suffering. Yet in the general scope of Scripture, we are told that it is because of sin that suffering and death came into the world. So there was a sound idea, at least partially, in the minds of the disciples. They at least understood that there is some kind of connection between moral evil and physical suffering. Jesus, however, took the opportunity to teach them that though, in general, there would be no suffering and there would be no death in the world if there were no sin in the world, we cannot conclude that everybody suffers in proportionate measure to the degree of their sin. The Bible makes it clear that that's not the case. There are the wicked who prosper and the righteous who suffer. The book of Job is designed to correct that misunderstanding and to show that Job was an incredibly upright man, and yet he was visited with untold misery and suffering. The error of his friends was to assume that because Job's suffering was so severe, Job must have been an incredible sinner.

John 9 and the book of Job indicate that there is no one-to-one correspondence between sin and suffering, but we should not then conclude that there is no relationship at all between sin and suffering. When the people asked Jesus about this incident in Galilee when Pilate mingled the blood of the worshipers with the sacrifices, Jesus said, "Do you think that these Galileans were worse sinners?" He is answering His own question. He's saying, "No, they're not worse sinners." Now you would expect Jesus to say: "Accidents happen. This had nothing to do with their sin." Or you might expect Him to say, "These people who were killed were totally innocent people, and it's just a dreadful calamity that took place." But no. Instead, He warns them: "No, I tell you; but unless you repent, you will all likewise perish" (Luke 13:3).

People do dreadful things to others. The terrorist works indiscriminately. He doesn't aim at military installments; he aims at the general public; he aims at children in order to terrorize as many people as he can. With respect to the relationship between the victim and the perpetrator, the victim is innocent. That's true, and we need to remember that. On the other hand, it is also true that when we look vertically in terms of our relationship to God, none of us are innocent before God. That's what Jesus is trying to communicate: "Unless you repent, you will all likewise perish." He's saying to these people: "You're asking Me the wrong questions. Instead of being horrified that a good God would allow this catastrophe to befall these innocent people in Galilee, the question you should be asking is, Why wasn't our blood spilled in Galilee?"

That's a hard saying. Jesus is trying to remind these people that there is no such thing as an innocent person. He's trying to communicate to us that the real amazing question is not the justice of God but the grace of God. We sing the well-known song lyrics "Amazing grace, how sweet the sound that saved a wretch like me." We sing that in church with great gusto but with very little belief. Do we believe that we are wretches who have been saved by the grace of God? Do we really believe that the favors we receive from the hand of God are unmerited, unearned, and undeserved? We should be asking, Why didn't our blood flow in that place? How did we escape? How could God, who is a good God, allow me, a sinner, to continue to enjoy all these benefits?

The next incident contained in this narrative is that of the eighteen people on whom a tower in Siloam fell and killed. "Do you think that they were worse offenders than all the others who lived in Jerusalem?" (Luke 13:4). They weren't any worse; they weren't any better. The question is how God can allow that to happen. Jesus' answer is hard. He's saying: "Why shouldn't God allow that to happen? The question you should be asking is why that temple doesn't fall on your head."

If you believe that we live by grace, that's the response you have to have. Sometimes it takes the hard saying of Jesus in a situation like this to get us to remember that we are not exempt from tragedy or suffering or calamity or injustice from the hands of people. But anything that befalls me from the hand of God that is painful, sorrowful, or grievous can never be seen as an act of injustice because God does not owe us freedom from tragedies. God does not owe us freedom from temples falling on our heads or towers burying us beneath their rubble because we are debtors before God who cannot repay. Jesus' warning is hard: "No, I tell you; but unless you repent, you will all likewise perish" (v. 5).

Jesus says that a necessary condition must be met here. "Unless" indicates something that has to take place for a consequence to follow. Unless "A" happens, "B" cannot occur, or unless "A," "B" will occur. In this case, Jesus said, "Unless there is repentance, you will all likewise perish." The only way to avoid perishing at the hands of God is repentance. So we can all look forward to towers falling on us or our blood being mingled with sacrifices unless we repent. It gets hard when you realize that even if we do repent, towers can still fall on our heads in this world. Yet if a person makes it safely through all of life, never has an automobile accident, never experiences a plane crash or a train wreck, or never has a house fall on his head, if he remains impenitent to his last day, a tower will crush him and he will perish. That's the hard saying of Christ.

Jesus is not being insensitive or thoughtless or trying to be harsh with His hearers, but He does have to jolt them and jolt us into looking at things from the eternal perspective. The only way that we can deal with tragedy and with calamity is to understand that behind the things that we experience in the here and now stands the eternal purpose of God. Remember the promise of God to His people, that on the last day, He will personally dry the tears from our eyes. When God dries our tears, they stay dry.

19

For Those Whom
the Father Has Given

John 17

When it comes to the hard sayings of Jesus, it seems that the last place we would expect to find one is in the prayers of Jesus, and most particularly when we read the magnificent High Priestly Prayer of Jesus in John 17. Here we have an intimate opportunity to eavesdrop on Jesus as He is performing His work of intercession not only for the disciples who were His at that time but for all His people who believe in Him. In that sense, Jesus is praying for us, if we have embraced the testimony of the Apostles.

The setting for this prayer is the night before Jesus was crucified. It takes place in the upper room on the occasion when Jesus celebrated the Passover for the last time with His disciples and when He instituted the Lord's Supper. It is a particularly important occasion. It's also the occasion when we have the most extensive discussion ever from the lips of Jesus on the person and work of the Holy Spirit—John 14, 15, and 16—a very important segment of our Lord's teaching for us.

Here is the section of the High Priestly Prayer that contains the hard saying:

"I have manifested your name to the people whom you gave me out of the world. Yours they were, and you gave them to me, and they have kept your word. Now they know that everything that you have given me is from you. For I have given them the words that you gave me, and they have received them and have come to know in truth that I came from you; and they have believed that you sent me. I am praying for them. I am not praying for the world but for those whom you have given me, for they are yours. All mine are yours, and yours are mine, and I am glorified in them. And I am no longer in the world, but they are in the world, and I am coming to you. Holy Father, keep them in your name, which you have given me, that they may be one, even as we are one. While I was with them, I kept them in your name, which you have given me. I have guarded them, and not one of them has been lost except the son of destruction, that the Scripture might be fulfilled. But now I am coming to you, and these things I speak in the world, that they may have my joy fulfilled in themselves. I have given them your word, and the world has hated them because they are not of the world, just as I am not of the world. I do not ask that you take them out of the world, but that you keep them from the evil one. They are not of the world, just as I am not of the world. Sanctify them in the truth; your word is truth." (17:6–17)

What's the problem with this? It's a wonderful prayer of intercession. It's very comforting and heartening to hear our Lord plead so passionately for the preservation of those whom the Father has given to Him.

The problem comes with this one little qualifying statement in verse 9: "I am praying for them"—that is, for those whom the Father had given Him—"I am not praying for the world." Jesus makes a clear and sharp distinction between those for whom He is praying and those for whom He is not praying. He is not interceding for everyone, but He's interceding only for the believers, for those whom the Father has given to Him.

This text becomes so controversial in church history over one of the most hotly disputed doctrines in Protestant theology and in the tradition of Reformation theology, and that is the doctrine known as *limited atonement*. It's the *L* in the famous acrostic TULIP that summarizes the five points of Calvinism. That acrostic has its roots in a controversy that emerged in the Netherlands among the Dutch Reformed.

A group that had been significantly influenced by the theology called Arminianism, after Jacob Arminius, protested against certain teachings of the Reformation focusing on the doctrine of election. This group, called Remonstrants, isolated five teachings of Calvinism that they disagreed with. A council in the city of Dort responded with its own five points answering those objections, which is where we get the five points of Calvinism. These points are as follows: total depravity, unconditional election, limited atonement, irresistible grace, and the perseverance of the saints. All five points have generated controversy, but the *L* in particular has done so.

Limited atonement is the doctrine that teaches that Jesus did not die for everybody, that He did not die on the cross for the sins of the whole world, but that He died on the cross only for the elect—for a particular, specified group of people whom God had chosen from the foundation of the world. The sacrifice that Christ offered on the cross was intended and designed to redeem them and them alone, not just anybody indiscriminately.

There are many people today who identify as so-called four-point Calvinists. This is particularly true in the dispensational community. Historic dispensationalism in America has grown out of a Reformed tradition, and many dispensational theologians and believers would readily affirm total depravity, unconditional election, irresistible grace, and perseverance of the saints. The one they balk at is limited atonement. Those who object to limited atonement want to insist that the purpose of the cross was to make salvation possible for every person in the world and that Jesus did die on the cross for all the sins of all the people throughout history.

There is another controversy that is closely related to this one, but it is not the same controversy; it is the debate over universalism versus particularism. Universalism teaches that all human beings are ultimately saved and that the basis of their salvation is the person and work of Christ. That is, the atonement that Christ made on the cross guarantees the salvation of every human being. Particularism teaches that not everybody is saved but only those who have faith in Christ. In the historic debate between Arminianism and Calvinism, or between dispensationalism and Reformed theology, Arminianism and dispensationalism strongly and consistently affirm particularism and deny universalism. Reformed theology, dispensational theology, and Arminian theology all agree that not everybody is saved because it seems abundantly clear in Scripture that there will be people who will be in hell and who will be lost ultimately.

The main question about the atonement has to do not with its value but with its design or scope. What was God's purpose in sending Christ into the world to die on the cross? Did God, from all eternity, intend to save everybody? If He did, what would that mean? Everybody would be saved, or else God's intents are completely frustrated by the affairs of men. If it was God's purpose to save the whole world, then that purpose was frustrated and God's plan of redemption would be a failure. The assumption that the person in the Reformed tradition makes here is that when God has a plan and a design and a purpose, it doesn't fail. He brings to pass what He intends to bring to pass. This is nowhere truer than with His plan of salvation. If it ends up that somebody goes to hell and that not everybody is saved, that can only mean that it was never God's intention to save everybody. It was His intention to save some people in this world, not all people.

Is the cross of Christ the end of redemption or a means to the end? If it's the end, then all God ever intended to do was to make salvation possible by providing a Savior and then leave the consequences and the results up to us. Or is the cross the means that God employed to accomplish His eternal purpose of saving His people? Reformed theology says the latter, that the purpose of Christ's coming into the world was to save the elect. The purpose for Christ's going to the cross, according to God's eternal plan, was to save the elect, and when Christ died, He laid down His life for His sheep. He did not lay down His life for everybody. The atonement that He made, He made for His sheep, and those who are not His sheep do not participate in that atonement. Now, that sounds harsh. That's a hard saying. That is what is meant by *limited atonement*. It is limited not in effect but in design. It is also known as *particular redemption* because it is aimed at particular individuals who have been elected before the foundation of the world by the Father.

That's what brings us back to the High Priestly Prayer, where we see Jesus speaking repeatedly of those who have come to Him in faith and who were given to Him by the Father. It was the Father who gave Christ a body of children, a body of believers, so that the Son of God would see the travail of His soul and be satisfied. Can you imagine Jesus' going to the cross, offering an atonement to the Father, and then hoping that somebody would make use of it while theoretically realizing that His death could be completely in vain? If you deny this concept of particular redemption, you would have to admit that it's theoretically possible that nobody would ever come to Christ and that He could have suffered all that He did for nothing.

That's not the purpose of God. God wouldn't hear of such a thing. God sent His Son to the cross to make an atonement that would work, that would be effective. Christ offered Himself as a sacrifice to satisfy the demands of God for those that the Father had given Him. Jesus also mentions here in John 17 that all that the Father had given Him came to Him. He goes on to say that not one of them was lost, "except the son of destruction" (v. 12), Judas, who was never a believer. In reality, how many of those whom the Father has given to Christ are lost? None. The reason that we take such comfort in the intercessory work of Christ is that not only does Christ atone for the sin of His people, not only does He lay down His life for His sheep, but then He prays daily as our High Priest and as our intercessor for our preservation, so that not one of His people for whom He has died will ever, ever be lost.

It is a great comfort to know that if you have faith, the only reason you have faith is because of the gift of God and because God, out of His great mercy, has given you to His Son, and that God will not allow anything to snatch you out of His hands. You have a Priest who has entered into the Holy of Holies, who has made an atonement, who has sprinkled His own blood on the mercy seat of the covenant throne of God, and who presents that sacrifice to the Father on your behalf, that you may never, ever be lost.

Jesus set out to save His people, and He accomplished His mission. He did it perfectly and effectively for all who are given to Him by the Father. God's purposes do not fail; His plan is effective. Perhaps you are troubled by the idea of some kind of limit to the atoning work of Christ. Rest assured that there is no limit to the atoning work of Christ and its benefits for you if you are a believer. There is a serious limit of the atonement for those who are not believers.

The difficulty here is not whether everybody is saved or not everybody is saved. We ought to agree that if God purposed from all eternity that all mankind would be saved, then all mankind would be saved. He certainly has the power and the authority to save the whole world if it would please Him to do so. That was not His plan. That was not His desire. His desire was to save some and thereby to show His mercy and His grace, and to pass over others and thereby to show His justice and His holiness. In both cases, the glory of God is made manifest and His holiness and greatness are vindicated, so that God displays in the cross both His justice and His mercy. Those whom He intended to save, He saves, and that is the occasion of our rejoicing.

20

The Inner Struggle

Romans 7

Paul's letter to the Romans is clearly the weightiest epistle that he wrote; it's often called his magnum opus. It is here that he delves extensively into the whole plan of redemption. In chapter 7, Paul is addressing the spiritual warfare that goes on in the life of the Christian. He speaks in personal terms of an enormous spiritual struggle. One of the great controversies that arises out of this passage is this: Is Paul speaking of his present experience as a Christian, or is he reflecting on his past life as an unbeliever?

This question became central to a controversy over whether it is possible for a Christian in this world and in this life to achieve such a level of sanctification as to reach moral perfection. Churches have embraced different views of holiness and have endorsed different approaches to this subject and different understandings of perfectionism. We will focus on the ultimate kind of perfectionism that teaches that there is a work of grace available to Christians by which a person can now, instantaneously, through the anointing of the Holy Ghost, become completely and utterly free from sin. Some traditions endorse this view, while classical theology and Reformed theology thoroughly repudiate and reject it.

To explore the controversy, we must turn to the text to see where the difficulties lie: Romans 7:13–25. In verses 13–14, Paul, referring to the law, says, "Did that which is good, then, bring death to me? By no means! It was sin, producing death in me through what is good, in order that sin might be shown to be sin, and through the commandment might become sinful beyond measure. For we know that the law is spiritual, but I am of the flesh, sold under sin."

Paul uses the present tense and declares, "I am of the flesh, sold under sin." This text is also used to justify a view of sanctification that allows for the so-called carnal Christian, who doesn't bring forth any fruit of righteousness in his life but remains in the flesh. When we use the word *carnal*, we mean "flesh" or "fleshy." In biblical categories, "flesh" doesn't necessarily refer to the physical body but refers to the old lifestyle of the fallen sin nature.

Since Paul describes himself as carnal—that is, "of the flesh"—some have concluded that Paul must be speaking about his previous condition. That is the normal description that the Apostle uses to describe the unregenerate person, the person who is still in his fallen state. Paul also adds the phrase "sold under sin." Paul frequently speaks of the unregenerate person as dead in sin and trespasses, as under sin, as in bondage to sin; it certainly sounds as though he's describing himself, at least in this portion of the text, in terms that he normally uses to describe the unconverted person.

Let's continue reading the text:

> For I do not understand my own actions. For I do not do what I want, but I do the very thing I hate. Now if I do what I do not want, I agree with the law, that it is good. So now it is no longer I who do it, but sin that dwells within me. For I know that nothing good dwells in me, that is, in my flesh. For I have the desire to do what is right, but not the ability to carry it out. For I do not do the good I want, but the evil I do not want is what I keep on doing. Now if I do what I do not want, it is no longer I who do it, but sin that dwells within me.
>
> So I find it to be a law that when I want to do right, evil lies close at hand. For I delight in the law of God, in my inner being, but I see in my members another law waging war against the law of my mind and making me captive to the law of sin that dwells in my members. Wretched man that I am! Who will deliver me from this body of death? Thanks be to God through Jesus Christ our Lord! So then, I myself serve the law of God with my mind, but with my flesh I serve the law of sin. (Rom. 7:15–25)

If you follow Paul's train of thought carefully, it seems that he is speaking almost like a schizophrenic. He speaks of this power of sin that abides in his life, the sin or the flesh that is within him. As a result of this, he says, "What I want to do, I don't do; what I do not want to do, I do." He experiences this conflict over his actions and his behavior.

If ever the Apostle Paul fails to tell the truth, it's here. He's using a manner of speaking when he says, "For I do not do the good I want, but the evil I do not want is what I keep on doing" (v. 19). That is to say, "I will to do one thing and I don't do it, and I will not to do something else and I do that." If you took those words just as they are, Paul would not be making a whole lot of sense, but this statement is not an error in Paul's writing. It's elliptical. Certain things are tacitly understood. Let me explain.

When Paul says that he continues doing what he doesn't want to do, why does he do it? Because he wants to. Why does he say that he doesn't do the good he wants? Why does he not do those things that he would do? He would not do them because he doesn't want to do them. What he's talking about is the conflict of desires going on in him. We who are in Christ all experience that. If you asked me, "R.C., do you want to sin?" I would say: "No, of course not. I can't wait to be free from sin. I can't wait to be in heaven, to be glorified, to never worry about sin again." You say, "Well, R.C., if you don't want to sin, why do you sin?" "Well, because I want to. That's the problem: I have mixed desires." What I mean when I say that "I don't want to sin" is that, all things being equal, I don't want to sin. I would like to be in the state of glorification and perfection that I have not yet achieved, all things being equal. But the reason that I continue to sin at times is that I still have sinful desires that are in my flesh.

Paul frequently makes the distinction in the New Testament between the old man (the unconverted person) and the new man (the new person in Christ who has been quickened and indwelled by the Holy Spirit). When we become new people at conversion, when we are quickened by the Holy Ghost, that conversion, that regeneration, that quickening does not immediately annihilate the old sin nature. Paul makes it clear that sanctification is a lifelong process, one that requires laboring in fear and trembling. It involves work and is a constant struggle against those sinful impulses that remain after conversion.

He gives us the comforting news that in the process of spiritual growth, in our progress of sanctification, the old man is being put to death day by day and the new man is growing stronger as we are growing in the Lord. This is one of the great ironies of human life. As we age spiritually as Christians, we also age physically. I wish I had known what I know now back when I was eighteen years old. It could have saved me an awful lot of trouble. But as I also grow old, I long more and more for my resurrected body because my earthly body is falling apart. My body is decaying. My body doesn't have the vigor, the robustness, the strength, or the health that I enjoyed when I was younger. That is one of the things that every human being has to struggle with—the slow disintegration and decay of the body.

What's the good side? Age can't hurt the soul. The longer we are in Christ, the more years of experience we have as Christians, the stronger the soul is becoming. On the one hand we're losing something with the loss of our strength and the loss of our physical health, but at the same time we're gaining something so much more important and so much more valuable with the increase of strength of the new man, of the inner person, of the spiritual nature.

If Paul were speaking of his former condition, would he be describing such warfare? The warfare that he's talking about is not characteristic of the unconverted person. The unconverted person is carnal altogether. That's all that the person is—flesh. That person does not have the Holy Spirit, does not have any impulse to real righteousness, and has no driving desire to please Christ or to please God. All that comes with conversion. In a real sense, our lives don't become complicated until we're converted. That's when the war is declared. That's when we have to enlist, and we enlist for the duration of the battle that goes on until we are ultimately victorious in heaven. Paul says, "I find it to be a law that when I want to do right, evil lies close at hand" (v. 21). Again, he's speaking in the present tense. The unconverted person has evil present in him but does not will to do good. The Christian has evil present in him, while at the same time, there is this disposition or inclination or will to do good. That's the heart of the conflict.

I think the passage settles it once and for all in verse 22: "For I delight in the law of God, in my inner being." Yes, I have this sin within me that struggles against my desire to obey God, but there is delight in the inward man that is pleased and desires to obey the law of God. No unconverted person is in that state. Therefore, Paul must be speaking of his present life.

Paul underlines the contrast and the conflict by saying: "But I see in my members another law waging war against the law of my mind and making me captive to the law of sin that dwells in my members. Wretched man that I am! Who will deliver me from this body of death? Thanks be to God through Jesus Christ our Lord!" (vv. 23–25). Now, there's some ambiguity about the phrase "Who will deliver me from this body of death?" What is he talking about when he refers to "this body of death"? Some commentators simply think that Paul is referring to his physical body, and he can't wait to be released from his physical body to enter heaven, which Paul says is better than our existence here but not as good as it will be when we are in the final state of the resurrected body. Paul wants to get rid of this physical body, and I don't blame him. But I don't think that's what Paul is talking about.

Another suggestion is that when Paul says, "Wretched man that I am! Who will deliver me from this body of death?" he is referring directly to the sin nature of the flesh, not a literal physical body. I think that's basically true, but not entirely true. I've been persuaded by some scholars who have researched a certain practice in the ancient world that Paul may be using as an illustration. It is argued that in the ancient world, one of the punishments for murder in certain cultures was to have the corpse of one's victim tied to his back until that victim was so putrefied and decayed that nothing but the skeleton was left. At that point, the murderer was released from it. Can you imagine anything more horrible than to have to walk around for days with a dead body strapped to your back? A body of death would reduce a person to wretchedness.

Paul is using the phrase in a metaphorical or illustrative sense, saying that this is what the Christian life is like. We are a new person, but we still have to carry this old nature around with us. Our dreadful sin nature is like a putrefying body of death that hasn't yet completely fallen off our backs but continues to torment us and cause us to be in this ongoing conflict. "Thanks be to God through Jesus Christ our Lord!" was the Apostle's final cry (v. 25). Paul does not leave us wallowing in the struggle or in despair, but chapter 7 moves directly to chapter 8, which is so triumphant in its promise of the victory of God's grace in the Christian life.

Romans, like the rest of Scripture, teaches that the presence of sin continues in our lives until we enter glory, though we experience freedom from the power and the curse of sin in Christ. Therefore, perfectionism in this life is biblically impossible, and those who hold to perfectionism end up denigrating the biblical teaching on sin and sanctification. They do one of two things, although they often attempt both of them. One of those things is to radically alter the full measure of the demands of God's law. We have to drag the law down to the level of external performance rather than heartfelt obedience. This was the error that the Pharisees made—they set up guardrails that allowed them to feel satisfied in their righteousness while never addressing the law's demands on their hearts. They had a superficial understanding of the full demands of God's commandments. For us to deceive ourselves into thinking that we are perfect, we would have to believe that we have loved the Lord with all our hearts and with all our minds and with all our strength. Who has ever done that for even five minutes?

The second mistake is like the first. In order for us to be persuaded that we have achieved perfection of any kind, we have to have an exaggerated view of our own performance. So we bring God's law down and bring our own performance up so that the two can meet. Either one of those is an extreme danger for Christian growth, and both of them together are basically fatal.

21

Vessels Prepared for Destruction

Romans 9

The passage we've come to now is one of the most difficult texts to deal with in all of Scripture, if not the most difficult; it's found in Paul's letter to the Romans in chapter 9. This is the chapter in which Paul deals with the election of Jacob and the passing over of Esau. The Apostle raises this question:

> What shall we say then? Is there injustice on God's part? By no means! For he says to Moses, "I will have mercy on whom I have mercy, and I will have compassion on whom I have compassion." So then it depends not on human will or exertion, but on God, who has mercy. For the Scripture says to Pharaoh, "For this very purpose I have raised you up, that I might show my power in you, and that my name might be proclaimed in all the earth." So then he has mercy on whomever he wills, and he hardens whomever he wills. (Rom. 9:14–18)

We've already examined the problem of the hardening of Pharaoh's heart in an earlier chapter, but we've included this portion of the text as background for the part that follows, where Paul continues in anticipation of objections to the doctrine of election:

You will say to me then, "Why does he still find fault? For who can resist his will?" But who are you, O man, to answer back to God? Will what is molded say to its molder, "Why have you made me like this?" Has the potter no right over the clay, to make out of the same lump one vessel for honorable use and another for dishonorable use? What if God, desiring to show his wrath and to make known his power, has endured with much patience vessels of wrath prepared for destruction, in order to make known the riches of his glory for vessels of mercy, which he has prepared beforehand for glory—even us whom he has called, not from the Jews only but also from the Gentiles? As indeed he says in Hosea,

"Those who were not my people I will call 'my people,'
 and her who was not beloved I will call 'beloved.'"
"And in the very place where it was said to them, 'You are not my people,'
 there they will be called 'sons of the living God.'" (vv. 19–26)

Is the Apostle saying that God creates human beings evil and then punishes them for the deeds they perform according to their nature? Does God, like the potter, take a piece of clay that, from the very beginning, is destined to destruction? Does He shape it and mold it according to that end and then condemn it to judgment? This is probably one of the scariest passages that we run up against because the text certainly seems to suggest that God creates people for His own purpose who are already wicked and then punishes them for acting out of the state in which they were made. Some have taken this text to mean exactly that, though they have been few in number throughout church history.

The typical understanding of this text is in reference to the broader context of the chapter, which deals with the election of Jacob rather than Esau by which God shows mercy to one sinner and passes over the other sinner, but both Jacob and Esau are considered in divine election as fallen sinners. One receives mercy, the other receives justice, and no one receives injustice. That's the problem that we're going to deal with. Let me first make a reference to the thinking of Martin Luther on this text. In *The Bondage of the Will*, Luther noted man's tendency to fashion God after his own image, imagining a God who hardens nobody, condemns nobody, and pities everybody. The god that we want to believe in is a god who is not only *sometimes* merciful but *always* merciful, a god who never condemns anybody and never hardens anybody.

Luther goes on to say that we cannot comprehend how a just God can condemn those who are born in sin and cannot help themselves but must by a necessity of their natural constitution continue in sin and remain children of wrath. Luther is saying that we cannot see how God can be just in this manner, to punish those who are born in sin and are only doing what comes naturally.

There is no doubt that the New Testament and the Old Testament teach uniformly that we are indeed born in sin and that we are born with a fallen nature. Furthermore, we sin according to that corrupt nature, and God indeed expresses His wrath and judgment on us even as we work out this sinful nature. The question is, How is God just as He does so?

Luther's answer is less than satisfactory but is nevertheless insightful. He said God is utterly incomprehensible in all His attributes, so His justice must be incomprehensible as well. We simply cannot understand God's justice because it cannot be understood. We could say that Luther hides behind the doctrine of the incomprehensibility of God, which teaches that though we know God in part, we do not know Him exhaustively and totally or comprehensively. It doesn't mean that we are completely ignorant of the character of God, but it means that His ways are not our ways and His ways are past finding out. There is a depth to the perfection of God that eludes us and our ability to understand.

The Bible makes it abundantly clear that God is altogether just, and we assume His justice even when we cannot penetrate it and cannot understand it in its fullest measure. Therefore, I don't think that Luther is simply dodging the issue here; rather, he is saying that it remains a mystery to us how God could be just and still hold people responsible for their fallen nature and then judge them accordingly.

We are born in sin because of Adam's sin, and the fall of humanity in Adam involves a judgment on the entire human race, the human race being represented by Adam in the fall. In chapter 5, Paul makes it clear that we, in fact, all did fall in Adam and that the condition that we call original sin is the judgment of God on Adam and his seed for the first transgression that was made. Adam represented the entire human race, and if he had passed his probation, God would have rewarded him and all his descendants, and nobody would ever be complaining about injustice. The problem is that Adam fell and, with Adam, we fell and are now born under the judgment for Adam's first sin.

The Bible seems to teach clearly that God created Adam unfallen. The question becomes, Did Adam, at the time of his creation, have a prior inclination to sin? If so, where did he get it? There are two primary ways to answer these questions, and each one has some mystery associated with it.

The first view is that God created Adam with some inclination to sin, yet those who hold this view nevertheless say that God is not unjust in doing so. It's mysterious to them how God could create a person with a disposition to sin, punish him for exercising that disposition, and still be just in doing it. The advantage of this position is that it clearly retains the sovereignty of God. It does, however, raise a question about the goodness of God.

The second view is that God created Adam without any disposition to sin. Those who hold this view then must answer the question, How could Adam have sinned? A host of theologians in church history have landed on this view, saying that we don't know how Adam could have sinned; we only know that he did sin and that God didn't make him sin. In that regard, God's goodness is preserved, but it raises the question about His sovereignty. So we're on the horns of a dilemma. Which view we take is going to raise a significant question about the character of God—either with respect to His justice or with respect to His sovereignty. Many people don't feel the weight of the dilemma and simply chalk up Adam's sin to free will. They haven't really wrestled with how free will is exercised.

Which view is Paul teaching in Romans 9? I think he's teaching the latter view—that God created Adam without an inclination to sin—because the context emphasizes the mercy of God on sinners. Pharaoh was judged for his sin after he was hardened, but he was a sinner before he was hardened. Paul states: "He has mercy on whomever he wills, and he hardens whomever he wills. You will say to me then, 'Why does he still find fault? For who can resist his will?'" (vv. 18–19). Paul responds with a question: "But who are you, O man, to answer back to God?" (v. 20). He then continues: "What if God, desiring to show his wrath and to make known his power, has endured with much patience vessels of wrath prepared for destruction?" (v. 22). God is manifesting a certain patience and long-suffering to people who are manifestly wicked, but Paul says that He prepared them for destruction.

In the broader context of Romans 9, Paul appeals to the book of Hosea, where God promises to make *a people* of a group who were not a people (vv. 25–26; see Hos. 2:23). This context has to do with God's being merciful to some within Israel and judging the rest. The basis for that judgment is that those who were of Israel, who were supposedly the holy people of God, were nevertheless wicked, and some of Israel, such as Esau, were not to receive God's saving grace. The emphasis in Hosea, as in Romans 9, is on God's mercy toward undeserving sinners and His sovereign freedom to extend that mercy to whomsoever He wills.

We who are Christians were once no people, but now by God's grace we are His people. We are the wild olive branch grafted into the root of the tree. We bring nothing to the table, nothing inherent that would make God be moved to include us in His kingdom. Our only hope is the riches of His glory, of His mercy that those who were no people by grace are called His people. That's what election is all about.

22

The Authority
of Apostolic Teaching

1 Corinthians 7

A short passage in 1 Corinthians contains several points that could be considered hard sayings. We're going to focus on one point that has to do with Apostolic authority. In this passage, Paul gives various instructions about Christian marriage and sets forth regulations by which we are to be governed in our marital relationships. He writes:

> To the married I give this charge (not I, but the Lord): the wife should not separate from her husband (but if she does, she should remain unmarried or else be reconciled to her husband), and the husband should not divorce his wife.
>
> To the rest I say (I, not the Lord) that if any brother has a wife who is an unbeliever, and she consents to live with him, he should not divorce her. If any woman has a husband who is an unbeliever, and he consents to live with her, she should not divorce him. For the unbelieving husband is made holy because of his wife, and the unbelieving wife is made holy because of her husband. Otherwise your children would be unclean, but as it is, they are holy. But if the unbelieving partner separates, let it be so. In such cases the brother or sister is not enslaved. God has called you to peace. (7:10–15)

Here the Apostle is giving a directive. He is setting forth an Apostolic principle for the church. But he does so in an interesting way, noting parenthetically in verse 12 who is speaking: "I, not the Lord." He's careful to say that the source or the origin of this particular rule is coming from himself and not from Christ. Notice the stark contrast between Paul's statement here to the statement he previously made in verse 10: "To the married I give this charge (not I, but the Lord)." There is a contrast between the two. In verse 10, Paul gives a commandment that he himself utters but indicates that the commandment is not his own but is a commandment from God. Then in verse 12, he says, "Now *I'm* telling you something, not the *Lord*."

What does it mean when Paul says that this is something he's saying and not the Lord? What does this do to the authority of the statement? There have been different approaches to this text. One of the most common ones is this: Since Paul goes out of his way to say that it is his own instruction and not the Lord's, this piece of instruction should be set apart in terms of authority from the rest of Scripture. Paul is speaking under his own authority rather than being guided by the Holy Spirit, the argument goes, so his words here are not inspired and do not carry with them the authority of God.

The term *Apostle* translates the Greek *apostolos*, which means "one who is sent." It is not that anybody who is sent is necessarily an Apostle. If I send my child to the grocery store for a loaf of bread, I don't therefore confer Apostolic status upon my child. In the Greek world, however, an Apostle functioned as an emissary for a king or for the government and had the vested authority to speak on behalf of the king or for the nation. We find this concept in the New Testament with respect to those men whom Christ selected to be His representatives. We are accustomed to speaking of disciples and Apostles as though the term *disciple* and the term *Apostle* were synonyms, but they are not. The word *disciple* means "learner," and Jesus had many disciples who were students in His rabbinic school.

On one occasion Jesus sent seventy of His disciples out on a particular mission. We read in John 6 that on another occasion when Jesus was teaching on a controversial issue and after He had given a hard saying, many of those who had been following Jesus and who had been disciples left Him. Jesus then turned to the Twelve and looked at Peter and asked, "Do you want to go away as well?" (v. 67). Peter responded: "Lord, to whom shall we go? You have the words of eternal life" (v. 68). Some of the wider group of disciples deserted Jesus, but His inner circle, the core group of twelve, remained. These men (with the exception of Judas) were appointed to be Apostles, and then Paul was added to this Apostolic group later. All the Apostles were also disciples, but not all the disciples were Apostles.

I used to ask my seminary students, "Who is the first Apostle in the New Testament?" Some might answer Mary the mother of Jesus or John the Baptist. But no, the first and chief Apostle of the New Testament is Jesus. He is the One sent from God. Jesus repeatedly declares this to His people, saying, "I speak nothing on My own authority, but I say only that which I have been authorized to say by the Father. Everything that the Father has told Me to say, I say," and so on. Jesus got into a dispute with the Pharisees because the Pharisees claimed to believe in the Father but rejected Jesus. Jesus disallowed that disjunction: "If you reject Me, you are rejecting the Father, because the Father sent Me." There is a close connection between the Apostle and the one who sent him. If you reject the Apostle, you reject the authority of the one who has authorized the Apostle to speak in his stead. Jesus, when He commissioned His Apostles, said to them, "Those who receive you receive Me, and those who do not receive you do not receive Me."

That's important for us to understand today, particularly in light of some of the controversies that rage in the church. Some people attempt to drive a wedge between Paul and Jesus and launch scurrilous attacks against the Apostle Paul, saying such things as this: "Jesus I love, and Jesus I obey, but I just can't stand Paul. He's narrow-minded and exclusivist." These attacks against Paul's authority are attacks on the authority of Christ, because elsewhere Paul labors the point that he is an Apostle, not by the will of men, not by flesh and blood, but through the call and authority of God. That's one of the reasons that the book of Acts narrates, more than once, the circumstances of Paul's conversion on the road to Damascus and the accompanying call by Christ to be an Apostle. When we are dealing with the Apostles, we're dealing with those who have been delegated authority from Christ.

We're also talking about the very foundation of the church. I would ask my seminary students, "What's the foundation of the Christian church?" They would usually answer, "Jesus is the foundation." But no, Jesus is not the foundation of the church. Jesus is the chief cornerstone. The Bible does say that no foundation can be laid except that which is laid in Christ Jesus. The foundation of the church, however, is the prophets and the Apostles. The whole building rests on the Apostolic word or the prophetic Word of God.

Given the understanding of this high level of Apostolic authority, what are we to do with this passage when Paul says, "To the rest I say (I, not the Lord)" (1 Cor. 7:12)? The first thing we notice about the text is that he's not saying that he's contradicting something that the Lord has said. Paul is not saying, "Jesus told you one thing, and now I'm going to tell you something else." But Paul is careful to point out that he apparently does not have this word that he's about to say by any conscious, direct communication from Christ.

At what level of authority do we put this passage? Those who believe in the inspiration of the Bible approach it in two different ways. The first way is to say that it doesn't matter whether Paul had it through direct communication from Christ. The fact that he is an Apostle still leaves us with the same authority as anything else that the Apostle says because his office as an Apostle is to speak for Christ, and so this is part of the inspired text and carries with it nothing less than the authority of God. The second way is to limit which parts of Paul's statement are inspired.

In connection with the first idea, it's important to note that the doctrine of inspiration—according to which we confess that the biblical authors were superintended by the Holy Spirit such that the words they wrote are the very words of God—does not mean that the Apostles were inspired in everything that they ever said or wrote. That is to say, not everything that they ever said over dinner or in the marketplace carried the weight of divine authority.

The Roman Catholic Church recognized the danger of getting this wrong when it laid out its exposition of papal infallibility at the First Vatican Council in 1870. The church was careful to restrict that infallibility so that when the pope is having a conversation over the dinner table, for instance, those words are not to be understood as perfect or infallible. Rather, infallibility is restricted to when the pope is speaking on matters *de fide*, or "with respect to the faith," and is speaking *ex cathedra*, or "from the chair," in a particularly formal, specific environment.

There were, of course, conflicts between the Apostles. In Galatians, when Paul was struggling with the Judaizing heresy, he made mention of Peter's vacillation on the issue and how he had to confront Peter over his behavior. The

Council of Jerusalem was called, in part, to settle a dispute among the Apostles over what was required of gentile believers. Obviously, they had ideas among themselves that were in conflict when they weren't working under the inspiration of the Spirit. The Apostles were not permanently or inherently infallible; their being inspired by the Spirit extends only to their work of writing Scripture. Nevertheless, in their writing Scripture, they carried Apostolic authority and were inspired by the Holy Spirit to write exactly what He wanted them to write.

The second way of approaching this text states that Paul's being inspired extends only to his statement that this is his idea and not the Lord's, and that inspiration does *not* extend to the actual content of Paul's teaching. In other words, Paul was saying under the superintendence of the Holy Spirit, "I want you to know, and I want you to know infallibly, that I'm teaching this to you fallibly." He means to instruct us not to take this admonition as being of divine authority.

I would favor the first view: that even though Paul is declaring here that he did not get this teaching through the immediate enlightenment of the Holy Spirit, nevertheless as an Apostle he's making a command. This command comes to us by virtue of Apostolic authority and by virtue of inspiration, even if Paul is not immediately aware of his own inspiration. That's another point that we need to understand. The prophets who prophesied in the Old Testament did not necessarily always understand the content of their own messages. That wasn't their responsibility. Their responsibility was to deliver the messages, and they didn't have to fully comprehend the messages themselves.

A later passage in 1 Corinthians sheds a little bit of light on this matter: "Or was it from you that the word of God came? Or are you the only ones it has reached? If anyone thinks that he is a prophet, or spiritual, he should acknowledge that the things I am writing to you are a command of the Lord. If anyone does not recognize this, he is not recognized" (14:36–38). Paul is saying to the Corinthians: "Remember the things that I am writing to you, the things that I am commanding you from the Lord." That doesn't necessarily mean that the earlier text is therefore turned around and now comes from the Lord. Paul may be just speaking elliptically here, saying, "Everything else that I've told you in this letter is from the Lord except that which I specifically designate as coming from myself."

The good news about this particular troublesome passage is that ultimately it really doesn't matter a whole lot because the instruction that Paul gives, that he says is a commandment that comes from him, at the very least comes from the Apostle and has been recognized by the church in all ages to carry Apostolic authority. Paul is adding something to the rules and regulations for marriage and divorce that was not explicitly spelled out by Jesus. He is making allowance for the separation of couples who find themselves in a marriage with an unbeliever.

We must be careful here. Paul does not endorse a Christian's marrying a non-Christian. The background is presumably that two non-Christians have been married and that at some point one of them became converted and the unconverted one wants out of the marriage. Paul is saying that the believer should not get rid of the unbeliever just because they're now in an unequally yoked marriage, but that if the unbeliever wants out, the believer is free to let that person out of the marriage and to be at peace about it. We can conclude that the Apostle, whether he got his information directly from Jesus or not, gives important instruction to the church, and the church submits to it.

We must remember that no writings that have been passed down to us in the Christian community today have come directly from the pen of Jesus. The inscripturating of the teaching of our Lord was entrusted to the Apostles. When we want to place Jesus against Paul or Paul against Jesus, we are trying to pit Paul against Luke or Paul against Mark or Paul against Matthew because all that we know of the teaching of Jesus comes to us through the Gospel writers. It's because of their delegated authority that we trust that we know the actual teachings of Jesus Christ. If we reject the authority of the Apostles, we reject the authority of Christ—and if we reject the authority of Christ, we reject the authority of God Himself.

23

To Cover
or Not to Cover

1 Corinthians 11

This next hard saying is important for several reasons, and frankly, for reasons far beyond the particular matter that is addressed in the text. I'm referring now to this question of women's wearing head coverings in church. I know that some churches get into great controversy about this, but for the most part in the church today, at least in the American church, that tradition of women's covering their heads in worship on Sunday morning has been abandoned.

The text that has provoked this question is 1 Corinthians 11:2–16. Paul begins by saying in verse 2, "Now I commend you because you remember me in everything and maintain the traditions even as I delivered them to you." The word "tradition" translates the Greek *paradosis*, meaning "that which is given across or given over." We know that Jesus was in frequent controversy with the Pharisees over the subject of tradition, but the tradition that Jesus rebuked and admonished was the tradition of men. When the Apostles speak of tradition, however, they're not talking about human tradition; rather, they're talking about that which has been handed over from the Apostles to the church, from the Old Testament to the New Testament, to that treasury of divine truth that had been passed on from generation to generation. These were not traditions that were to be negotiated. This is God's tradition. But here Paul is speaking about keeping the traditions as he had delivered them; he's speaking of an Apostolic tradition.

Paul goes on:

> But I want you to understand that the head of every man is Christ, the head of a wife is her husband, and the head of Christ is God. Every man who prays or prophesies with his head covered dishonors his head, but every wife who prays or prophesies with her head uncovered dishonors her head, since it is the same as if her head were shaven. For if a wife will not cover her head, then she should cut her hair short. But since it is disgraceful for a wife to cut off her hair or shave her head, let her cover her head. For a man ought not to cover his head, since he is the image and glory of God, but woman is the glory of man. For man was not made from woman, but woman from man. Neither was man created for woman, but woman for man. That is why a wife ought to have a symbol of authority on her head, because of the angels. Nevertheless, in the Lord woman is not independent of man nor man of woman; for as woman was made from man, so man is now born of woman. And all things are from God. Judge for yourselves: is it proper for a wife to pray to God with her head uncovered? Does not nature itself teach you that if a man wears long hair it is a disgrace for him, but if a woman has long hair, it is her glory? For her hair is given to her for a covering. If anyone is inclined to be contentious, we have no such practice, nor do the churches of God. (vv. 3–16)

This passage is replete with difficulties for us, living in the modern world far removed from the situation of the Corinthian congregation, and it raises a bigger question than the immediate question of head coverings. The question is this: What is the Christian's obligation with respect to keeping customs that were kept in biblical times?

Virtually every biblical scholar recognizes the distinction between principle and custom. Principles are those commands of God that apply to all people at all times in every culture. Customs are those things that are variant local applications of principle. For example, the principle of tithing is in the New Testament, and in those days, it was done through the denarius or the shekel or whatever currency was used. Does that mean that the only way we can please God today is by paying our tithes in shekels or denarii? Of course not. The monetary unit was customary. Things such as monetary units and clothing styles are subject to change from culture to culture, from place to place. Many times, distinguishing between custom and principle is a relatively easy matter, but not always.

Here is a guideline to use if you can't decide whether something's a custom or principle: Whatever is not of faith is sin. This means the burden of proof is always going to be on those who argue that such and such a command is custom and not principle. If you're not sure, then applying the guideline means that you should treat it as a principle because if you treat a custom as a principle, the only guilt you bear is for being overscrupulous, but if you take a principle of God and treat it as a local custom and don't observe it, you have sinned against God.

Regarding this text about head coverings, different positions have been taken by scholars and theologians, and they address three different aspects to the passage: women ought to cover their heads (in some translations, to cover their hair) with a veil as a sign of the woman's submission or subordination to her husband. The three aspects are that the woman is supposed to cover her head, cover it with a veil, and cover it as a sign of submissiveness to her husband. Here are the different options for understanding this passage.

The first position states that all those things are customs—that's all. That is, in the early church it was part of the culture for women to be in submission to their husbands, and therefore the idea of wives' being submissive to their husbands is not principial and does not apply to all Christians in all times and places. Many people today take this approach. Since the basic thing that is being symbolized is a custom, then obviously the symbol is a custom and the means by which the symbol is demonstrated is a custom. Therefore, none of it is binding on us today.

The second position is that all of it is principial and applies to all Christians of all times and of all ages. Christian women should always be willing to show submissiveness and subordination to their husbands in church, and they should always and everywhere do it by covering their hair, and they should always and everywhere do it by covering their hair with a veil. There are Christian communities today that insist that women wear veils in obedience to this passage because they believe that all of it is principial, so Christians must obey all of it.

Between these two positions are middle-ground positions. The more common one among evangelicals, at least, is this: what is principial in this passage is the perennial responsibility of wives to be in submission to their husbands. That principle is articulated again and again in Scripture, and that principle abides. The symbol to indicate that submission is customary, however, so if one culture does it by having women cover their hair, another culture can do it some other way. It's not necessary to cover the hair because the covering of the hair is customary.

The fourth position can be found in many commentaries on 1 Corinthians, and it has to do with the context in Corinth. We know that Corinth, which was a commercial center of the ancient world, was a city with brothels and widespread prostitution. One of the signs of the prostitute was an uncovered head. Paul is telling the Corinthian ladies: "Don't come to church looking like prostitutes. In this environment, it's a scandal to be in a public place with your head uncovered, so Christians ought to be careful and not give the appearance of evil." Because our context is not the same as the original context, women nowadays do not have to observe this practice.

Here's the problem with that. I don't doubt for a minute that there was a problem with prostitutes in Corinth. Nor do I think that it's improper, when we don't know why a certain mandate is given in Scripture, to examine the cultural situation in order to gain clues for understanding certain admonitions. The problem is that this view assigns to Paul reasons for his saying something that are different from the ones that he himself gives. Paul does not leave us without a rationale for covering the head. Rather, he appeals to creation when he appeals to the distinction between man and woman. If anything transcends local custom, it is those things that are rooted in creation. That's why I'm very concerned to be loose with this passage because the Apostle doesn't say to keep your heads covered for fear of being mistaken for a prostitute. He appeals to creation. He says that a woman is given her hair as a "covering" as part of "her glory" (v. 15). If there's an idea that is foreign to our culture, it's this, as well as this statement of Paul's: "Does not nature itself teach you that if a man wears long hair it is a disgrace for him?" (v. 14).

This passage doesn't tend to sit well with modern American youth. In the 1960s, with all the societal changes that were going on, men started wearing their hair down to their shoulders and even beyond that. The interesting thing is what happened to women's hairstyles. The women at that time started wearing their hair down to their waists. It's almost like there was an unconscious battle to retain their sexual identity. It's interesting to watch how hairstyles change and this give-and-take between the sexes. When I was in high school, the thing to do was to wear a crew cut. For years I wore a crew cut, and the girls wore short-cropped hairdos such as a bob. As women's hairstyles became shorter, men's hairstyles got shorter yet, and vice versa. Paul states that it's a shame for a man to have long hair, so you have to ask the obvious question: How long is long? "Long" is a relative term, and it's got to be related to some norm or standard. The only norm that makes sense to me is the length of women's hair. When Paul says that it's a shame for men to have long hair, he must mean in comparison to women.

What does Paul mean about the woman's hair being her glory? He appeals to creation. In creation, man is given the superordinate role. He's not superior to woman, but he's given the position of leadership. The woman is given the position of subordination. Is there any compensation for that? Yes, she gets a special glory that the man doesn't get. That glory, strange as it may sound to our ears, is related to her hair. Her hair becomes the symbol of the added glory with which God adorns the woman. It's no small thing to recognize that it has been a persistent thing that culture after culture has regarded the female gender of the human species as the fairer sex. If you look in the animal kingdom, the male of a given species is usually more brightly colored or more showily adorned. Consider the male lion and the female lion. The male lion is the one with the mane. Think of pheasants or cardinals. If you look at birds and various animals, traditionally it's the male that gets the special adornment. But not with humans. With us, the beauty is focused on the woman. That's her glory, and it's symbolized by her hair, which identifies her as a woman. One of the ways that we have historically and classically been able from a distance to identify a woman is by her hair.

Paul says to women that when they come into the church, they should cover that glory, cover it as a sign of submission. Then he says that they should do so "because of the angels" (v. 10). Some have made bizarre interpretations of this phrase, saying that women must cover their hair lest they tempt the angels, and that if the women don't have their beautiful glory covered, the angels are going to be tempted to come down and seduce them. This is nonsense. The point of the phrase "because of the angels" is to emphasize that when we come together in solemn worship and in the assembly of the saints, we come before the very presence of Christ and before the throne of God and the whole host of heaven. In that heavenly sphere, there is an order that is established. The angels subordinate themselves to Christ. Christ subordinates Himself to His Head, the Father in heaven. Man, who is made in the image of God, is called to subordinate himself to the heavenly powers, and the wife is supposed to show her submission to this whole cosmic order of the authority of God, of Christ, and of the host of heaven.

I realize that styles and fashion change, that people today are not particularly scrupulous about this business of covering their heads, and that women today who come to church with their heads uncovered are not coming as an act of protest against the order of the universe or against the authority of Christ or even of their submission to their husbands. I don't think that's what's behind all this. It does concern me, however, that the custom of the woman's covering her head in America did not pass away until we saw a cultural revolt against the authority of the husband over the wife, not just in the home or in the church but in the whole of culture. It frightens me that we're taking our cue not from the Scriptures but from the culture or the fashions where we live.

I know scholars for whom I have the utmost respect who disagree with me completely on this text. I don't want to be dogmatic about it. My view is that Paul is appealing to creation and that Paul is saying that women ought to cover their heads. This is not the article on which the church stands or falls, but I think that we should seek to be faithful in small things, that we may be prepared to be faithful in many things. At the very least, it was important enough for the Apostle Paul to include it in his instructions to the church.

If you are a woman who has read this chapter today, let me ask you please not to simply react to me or to Paul in this passage but to think of the deeper question involved here, which is far beyond the issue of head coverings. Do we not (and I should certainly also include the men in this) understand that to come into the presence of God is a sacred thing? We have done all kinds of things in our culture to desacralize worship. I realize that we can worship God anywhere—outside, in a barroom if we need to—but we ought to bring a certain attitude or demeanor with us when we come into the presence of God, particularly for the purpose of corporate worship. I'm dismayed that our worship has become more and more casual. When that takes place, our adoration for the One we have come to worship and our submission to His authority and to His will begin to be compromised. I urge you to understand this difficult text in light of that higher question.

24

The Rapture
of the Church

1 Thessalonians 4

When I was a little boy, my aunt lived in our home with us. Every day, she listened to Kathryn Kuhlman, a famous faith healer and radio preacher. She would say, "I want you to know that as long as God is still on His throne and your faith is still intact, everything is going to turn out all right." Later on, she became nationally famous when she not only had her healing services in Pittsburgh but also held them in Los Angeles and had a national television program. She was the mentor of Benny Hinn, the television faith healer.

I met Kathryn Kuhlman once at her office in Pittsburgh. As she gave us a tour, she came to what seemed to be a large closet. She unlocked the door and opened it, and inside were shelves and shelves filled with the radio tapes of her ministry. She then told me why she kept them there. She said that they were in a metal-lined vault so that they would be preserved for those left behind on earth during the rapture. Those people would be able to hear the teachings of the New Testament when there won't be any Christians around to teach them. That was a fascinating rationale.

The rapture has become a popular theme in Christian culture. Perhaps you've seen the bumper sticker that reads, "In case of rapture, this vehicle will be unmanned." Hal Lindsey's book *The Late Great Planet Earth* popularized the idea of the rapture. In recent decades, the *Left Behind* series of books has sold millions of copies.

The popular idea of the rapture is that a moment is coming, perhaps soon, when Christians will suddenly be caught up in the air, disappear from sight, and have a secret rendezvous with Christ in the clouds. This theory is also known as the secret rapture, and it holds that Christ will whisk believers away for a certain time before returning again. This theory postulates not one return of Christ at the end of the age but two, and arguments persist among believers about the timing of the secret rapture, especially in relation to the postulated great tribulation that they believe will come upon the earth before the consummation of Christ's kingdom. Many believe in what is called the pretribulation rapture—that is, the rapture will happen before the great tribulation. Christ will first come and remove all believers from the earth so that they will not have to endure any of the pain and persecution associated with this great tribulation. Others argue that this tribulation period will run seven years and that the rapture will occur in the middle of that seven-year tribulation after three and a half years of extreme persecution of the Christian community have transpired; this view is known as the midtribulation rapture. Finally, there are those who argue that the rapture will not occur until after the seven years of tribulation, and this is obviously referred to as the posttribulation view.

This concept of a rapture comes from another hard saying from the New Testament. In 1 Thessalonians 4, Paul writes this:

> But we do not want you to be uninformed, brothers, about those who are asleep, that you may not grieve as others do who have no hope. For since we believe that Jesus died and rose again, even so, through Jesus, God will bring with him those who have fallen asleep. For this we declare to you by a word from the Lord, that we who are alive, who are left until the coming of the Lord, will not precede those who have fallen asleep. For the Lord himself will descend from heaven with a cry of command, with the voice of an archangel, and with the sound of the trumpet of God. And the dead in Christ will rise first. Then we who are alive, who are left, will be caught up together with them in the clouds to meet the Lord in the air, and so we will always be with the Lord. Therefore encourage one another with these words. (vv. 13–18)

This very brief passage is filled with a number of significant things. Paul introduces this description of the rapture by expressing his purpose for teaching the church these things. He says, "We do not want you to be uninformed" (v. 13). Uninformed about what? With respect to those believers who have fallen asleep, which is a reference to those who have already died. The question that Paul is addressing is this: What happens to those believers who die before Christ returns? Will they miss this marvelous event of the consummation of the kingdom of Christ when Christ appears in glory? Paul says that though those of us who are believers today haven't had the opportunity to be eyewitnesses of the life of Jesus, there will be one redemptive-historical moment that every believer will be able to witness with his or her own eyes: His coming again in glory.

You can understand why the people in the first-generation church were concerned about this. Jesus had left, and He said that He was going to come back in glory. Those who waited for the fulfillment of that promise and died before it was consummated left their friends and relatives with this obvious question: Are they going to miss out on this event, and are those who are alive at the time of the second coming to be the only ones who enjoy this spectacle of the exalted glory of Christ? Paul begins to answer that question by saying, "We do not want you to be uninformed." The word he uses there, which is sometimes translated as "ignorant," is *agnostos*, from which we get the word *agnostic*. Paul doesn't want the Thessalonians to be without knowledge, so he announces to them that he is prepared to give them the answer to this question, an answer that he says he has received immediately and directly from Christ Himself.

Paul goes on: "For this we declare to you by a word from the Lord, that we who are alive, who are left until the coming of the Lord, will not precede those who have fallen asleep" (v. 15). Paul turns the tables on the question. People assumed that those who were alive at the time of Christ's appearance would have the advantage over those who perished before the return of Jesus, and Paul is saying that this is not the case at all. Rather, if anybody has the advantage, it will be those who perished before Christ's return because they will precede us to this magnificent event in their resurrection. Verses 16–17 say: "For the Lord himself will descend from heaven with a cry of command, with the voice of an archangel, and with the sound of the trumpet of God.

And the dead in Christ will rise first. Then we who are alive, who are left, will be caught up together with them in the clouds to meet the Lord in the air." The firstfruits of those who will enjoy the reunion with the returning Christ will be the dead in Christ, who will be raised from the dead and caught up into the air first, and then those who are alive at the time will be caught up into the air to join Christ, along with their resurrected brothers and sisters.

I've always been puzzled by the idea of a secret rapture as taught by Kathryn Kuhlman and the *Left Behind* series. If it's going to be a secret, it will be the worst-kept secret in all of history, because the imagery that the Apostle uses here is that of Christ's appearing in clouds of glory with the shout of the archangel and the sound of the trumpet of God, like the shofar in the Old Testament. The shofar was a loud blast from the ram's horn that announced a solemn assembly and the congregational gathering. For this to happen in secret would require that the resurrection be invisible, the translation of the saints be invisible, and the unbeliever be deaf to the sounds of the trumpet and the shout of the archangel and blind to the manifestation of the shekinah glory of Christ. In other words, everything in this text suggests a public spectacle of the highest magnitude that nobody could possibly miss. There will be no secret to it whatsoever.

Whence comes the idea that there are going to be two returns and that all of this will take place because the church is going to avoid the tribulation? When the tribulation is announced in Jesus' teaching in Matthew's gospel, Jesus talks about these grim days of great affliction but states that the days will be shortened for the elect's sake. This suggests that afflictions will be temporary so that the believers who are enduring it will be able to survive it, not that we will escape it altogether. There's no need to postulate two separate comings of Jesus. The primary error here is the assumption that the rapture involves people's being removed from this planet and then taken up to be hidden with Christ for another three and a half or seven years, which the Bible never says anywhere.

How, then, do we understand the language of this text? What is the purpose of people's being taken up into the air to meet Jesus? The key to understanding this is to understand the imagery of the first-century community. In the ancient world, the Roman legions would go away and be gone for three or four years in their conquests, as Julius Caesar records in his *Gallic*

Wars. When they went into battle, they would carry banners with the letters SPQR, meaning *Senatus Populusque Romanus*, or "the senate and people of Rome." The understanding was that the Roman armies were representing the senate and the Roman people. After they conquered a nation, they would bring some of the leading captives back in chains, along with all kinds of spoil and plunder from the vanquished nations. When they returned to Rome in victory, they would camp about a mile outside the city, and an envoy would come into the senate to announce that the troops were back and that they were victorious. Immediately, preparations were made for the triumphal entry of the Roman soldiers back into the city square. An arch would be quickly built to commemorate the triumph. The city would also be adorned with garlands and with perfumes, chiefly to subdue the odor of these sweaty slaves that they were bringing and would be a sweet aroma wafting through the streets of Rome. After everything was prepared, everyone who was a citizen of the city of Rome was notified by a signal from the trumpeter of the Roman legions that the triumphal procession was about to begin. The Roman citizens then left the city and went out and joined the gathered soldiers and marched together with them back into the city through the arch, participating in the victory of their armies.

The Apostle is using this exact imagery for the triumphal return of Christ. The purpose of the rapture is not to vacate the earth of saints. The purpose of the rapture is not for Jesus to hover in the air with them for three and a half or seven years and come back a second time. As Paul states in Thessalonians, the purpose is for the saints to meet Him in the air as He is descending on the clouds of glory before He touches down to lay claim to this world that He has conquered. First, the dead in Christ are raised to meet Him in the air and to become part of His triumphal entourage. Then the believers who are alive are also caught up to be part of the procession as it descends to the earth. This is not a removal of the church from this world for any period of time, but it is the church's meeting Christ to participate in His exaltation, a theme that Paul preaches again and again—that if we are marked by baptism, we are marked not only with the humiliation of Jesus but with the exaltation of Christ, that we who participate in His sufferings will also participate in His glory, and that we will all be there to be part of the army of Christ as it returns in triumph from heaven to this earth. Paul concludes this brief narrative by saying,

"Encourage one another with these words" (v. 18). He tells the Thessalonians to take courage, to be comforted by the sure promise of Christ that we will participate with Him when He returns in honor and in glory.

I have no desire to scare anybody with the idea that we as Christians may have to pass through a severe tribulation before we enjoy the exaltation of Christ. But the warnings that come in the New Testament are sober, and in every age the church is called to be prepared to endure great affliction and great suffering. It's important for us to understand that such a persecution could erupt in our day, and we need not be caught off guard.

25

The Man
of Lawlessness

2 Thessalonians 2

In the previous chapter, we looked at the rapture, and I mentioned the theory of the pretribulation rapture that has become popular in the Christian subculture. I now want to direct our attention to another text that touches on that idea.

In 2 Thessalonians 2:1–4, Paul writes:

> Now concerning the coming of our Lord Jesus Christ and our being gathered together to him, we ask you, brothers, not to be quickly shaken in mind or alarmed, either by a spirit or a spoken word, or a letter seeming to be from us, to the effect that the day of the Lord has come. Let no one deceive you in any way. For that day will not come, unless the rebellion comes first, and the man of lawlessness is revealed, the son of destruction, who opposes and exalts himself against every so-called god or object of worship, so that he takes his seat in the temple of God, proclaiming himself to be God.

Paul is trying to combat a rumor that had obviously been circulated among the Thessalonians by somebody claiming to quote the Apostle Paul. The rumor was to the effect that the day of the Lord had already come and that they had missed this appearance of Christ and the gathering of His people—that is, the rapture. So Paul warns the Thessalonians against being deceived and says something that's extremely important—namely, that there are things that must happen before that day of the Lord will take place. Let's see what Paul says those things are.

Beginning in verse 3, Paul states, "For that day will not come, unless the rebellion comes first." This rebellion, or what some translations call "falling away," is usually described as the "great apostasy." Next, Paul says that "the man of lawlessness is revealed, the son of destruction," so we know that this experience of the rapture will not take place unless or until the man of lawlessness is revealed. This man of lawlessness "opposes and exalts himself against every so-called god or object of worship, so that he takes his seat in the temple of God, proclaiming himself to be God." Here is a descriptive sequence of this man of lawlessness, who is often identified with the figure of the antichrist.

The term *antichrist* is capable of two senses, both of which may be, and I think should be, applied to one individual. The word in Greek is *antichristus*. The prefix *anti-* has two distinct meanings. One is "against." For example, when we have arguments, we say that those opposed to a particular thesis are *anti* that thesis. But the term *anti-* can also mean "in the place of." Therefore, the antichrist could be considered, on the one hand, a figure who stands clearly opposed to or against Christ. But on the other hand, the antichrist is someone who seeks to be a substitute for Christ.

Both ideas are incorporated in this description of the man of lawlessness, the son of destruction, who tries to oppose Christ and also be a false christ himself, a substitute christ who tries to replace the role of God by setting himself up with divine authority in the temple and so on. We find both meanings of the Greek prefix incorporated in this description of the man of lawlessness. He both opposes Christ and exalts himself above all that is called God and all that is truly worshiped in order to seat himself as God in the temple of God, portraying himself as God.

Paul continues in verses 5–12:

Do you not remember that when I was still with you I told you these things? And you know what is restraining him now so that he may be revealed in his time. For the mystery of lawlessness is already at work. Only he who now restrains it will do so until he is out of the way. And then the lawless one will be revealed, whom the Lord Jesus will kill with the breath of his mouth and bring to nothing by the appearance of his coming. The coming of the lawless one is by the activity of Satan with all power and false signs and wonders, and with all wicked deception for those who are perishing, because they refused to love the truth and so be saved. Therefore God sends them a strong delusion, so that they may believe what is false, in order that all may be condemned who did not believe the truth but had pleasure in unrighteousness.

We could have a whole series of hard sayings just on the issues raised in this passage. For example, one of the most disputed questions in theology is whether Satan has the power to perform true miracles, because here Paul speaks about the "false signs and wonders" that are performed by this man of lawlessness (v. 9). Another question is why God would purposely send a delusion upon people, why God Himself would providentially send this worker of false signs and wonders. But the big enigma that we find in this text is the question of the identity of "he who now restrains" (v. 7).

Paul states that the man of lawlessness cannot be made manifest until the "he who now restrains it [i.e., lawlessness] . . . is out of the way" (v. 7). Who is this restrainer? I once read a commentary on Thessalonians written by Harry Ironside, who was important in the development of dispensationalism, the theological framework within which we frequently find advocacy for the pretribulation rapture. I was intrigued by Professor Ironside's argument. He argued that we know that the church will never have to go through a period of tribulation because 2 Thessalonians 2 teaches that before the tribulation takes place, the church will be taken out of the world. As I look at this text, I find it difficult to see anything to suggest that the church will be taken out of the world before the unleashing of the antichrist and the great tribulation. So how does Ironside support that theory? He makes some assumptions in his argument. The first is that the restrainer must be the Holy Spirit because it is the Spirit of God who keeps evil in check. The second is that if the restrainer is the Holy Spirit and the Holy Spirit is the One who restrains the man of lawlessness, and if the man of lawlessness cannot be revealed until the restrainer is removed, this would mean that the Holy Spirit would have to be taken away before the antichrist could come and the tribulation ensue. Where do we find the chief presence of the Holy Spirit in the world? We find the Holy Spirit indwelling every Christian. So if the restrainer is to be taken away, the only way we can take the restrainer away, if indeed the restrainer is the Holy Ghost, is to take the church, all the Christians, out of the world. Therefore, Ironside concludes, the church will be raptured before the manifestation of the man of lawlessness.

This is speculation in my judgment, and it rests on some very shaky assumptions. In the first place, the Apostle nowhere directly identifies the restrainer with the Holy Spirit. For the sake of argument, however, let's assume that the restrainer is the Holy Spirit. All that Paul would have to be saying is that the restraining power of the Holy Spirit would have to be removed from checking the progress of the antichrist. It doesn't mean that the church has to be removed and that the Holy Spirit has to be totally removed from the earth. Ironside is assuming that the church would have to be removed because, otherwise, the Holy Spirit would still be here. Let's follow his argument to its logical conclusion. If, indeed, the Holy Spirit must be totally removed from the world, not only would the church have to leave, but everybody else would also have to leave. Am I suggesting that pagans have the Holy Spirit? Yes, I am. They do not have the Holy Spirit in a salvific way, not in the sense of being indwelt or regenerated by the power of the Holy Spirit, but the Scriptures elsewhere make it clear that only by the Holy Spirit can any of us live at all. The power of life itself is rooted and grounded in the Holy Spirit, so that if the Holy Spirit were completely removed from the earth, all life would be removed with it. There would be no one around to endure a tribulation; even the man of lawlessness would have to fall over dead because he lives only through the sustaining power of God's Spirit.

The second thing to note is that Paul does not specifically identify the restrainer. Outstanding interpreters of Scripture throughout the centuries have wrestled with this text and have advanced several different possibilities for the identity of the restrainer. One possibility is that it is God the Father because it is by His common grace that all restraint on sin is directed toward the world; we can't remove God from the world completely, or the world itself would disappear. Another option that has been presented is that the restrainer of the man of lawlessness is the state because one of the functions of the state, as Paul develops in Romans 13, is to restrain evil. Perhaps the state becomes demonized and totally corrupt or it loses its governing authority. For example, suppose that Paul has in view here the Roman state, and suppose that something were to happen in the Roman order of government whereby certain restrictions and restraints were placed on its emperors by the Senate. Suppose that an emperor emerged who abolished the power of the Senate, usurped the authority to himself, claimed to be divine, and then began to wield unrestrained power; then the restraint of the Senate would be removed. Maybe that's what Paul has in mind. In fact, historically, many have argued this very point. Another possibility is that Paul is seeing himself as the restrainer of the man of lawlessness because he sees his ministry as one that checks the advance of unbridled wickedness, and he's thinking that maybe he will be removed from the scene and that when he is removed, then all hell will literally break loose. The reason that there are so many alternative views is that Paul does not identify the restrainer, so we are left to speculate. I think the text is sufficiently unclear at this point that it is difficult to construct a whole theory of the role of the antichrist and the time of the rapture based on the identity of the restrainer.

One of the interesting footnotes to this text that we've looked at here is that it seems that Paul was aware that his readers would know to whom he was referring when he talked about the one who restrained because he reminds them that he had talked about this with them when he had been in their midst. The Thessalonians enjoyed a certain amount of knowledge about this question that, in the providence of God, Paul was not concerned to give to us. The other thing that is important for us to understand is that Paul indicates that this mystery of iniquity was already at work. That's why many people believe that Paul was describing an event that was to take place soon, in the first century, although others have argued that the spirit of antichrist is multiple and there are many antichrists in the world, and the threat of antichrist is in every generation throughout the history of the church. In the meantime, however, let us learn that one thing is clear: God restrains the work of the antichrist. God is in control of the day and the hour of his manifestation, and our trust and our comfort must be in Him.

26

The Danger of Apostasy

Hebrews 6

One of the hard sayings of Jesus that has provoked so much consternation among Christians was Jesus' teaching concerning the unpardonable sin or blasphemy against the Holy Spirit (see chapter 15). The problem I want to address here is one that is often related to that teaching, but it is not identical to it. It's a problem that we find in the sixth chapter of the book of Hebrews.

I've always said that if I were locked up in prison and could have only one book of the Bible with me, I would want it to be the book of Hebrews. That's how highly I regard and love that book. Part of the reason I would want to have that book with me is that it gives such a wonderful recapitulation of the essence of the Old Testament as well as all the glorious teaching of the New Testament, and they're all conjoined together in that book.

Yet one of the remarkable points of church history is that it was disputed whether Hebrews was truly an Apostolic writing. The early church sought to discern which of the writings that had survived the Apostolic age were genuinely Apostolic and which were apocryphal or fraudulent. In the second century, a plethora of literature was produced by a heretical group known as Gnostics who tried to pass off their literature as Apostolic. So the church had to study this matter and debate which of the books were clearly Apostolic.

One of the books that was debated was the book of Hebrews. It was debated mainly because of what Hebrews teaches in the sixth chapter, which we will be addressing here.

The controversy that attends the sixth chapter of Hebrews is no small matter. It was one that the early church itself had to struggle with, and one of the ironies of that historical period is that the thing that made it decisive that Hebrews ought to be included in the New Testament canon was the church's conviction that it had been written by the Apostle Paul. Yet in today's environment in modern New Testament scholarship, few would argue that Paul wrote Hebrews. No one is saying that Hebrews isn't Apostolic; they simply think it was written by someone other than Paul, perhaps Apollos or Luke or Barnabas. Everybody recognizes the magnificent literary achievement that it is, but still, almost no one today believes that Paul wrote Hebrews. In fact, the only person I know who still believes that Paul wrote Hebrews is me. Why I believe he wrote the book is for another discussion, but suffice it to say, I do think Paul wrote Hebrews, and we will see in a few moments that the question of authorship is very important to understanding this problematic text.

Let's look at the text that has caused so much controversy and jump right into the hard saying. Hebrews 6:4–6 says, "For it is impossible, in the case of those who have once been enlightened, who have tasted the heavenly gift, and have shared in the Holy Spirit, and have tasted the goodness of the word of God and the powers of the age to come, and then have fallen away, to restore them again to repentance, since they are crucifying once again the Son of God to their own harm and holding him up to contempt."

This hard saying deals with the problem of apostasy. Apostasy is not the same thing as paganism. An apostate is distinguished from a pagan in this regard: the pagan has never made any profession of faith or any pretense of being a believer, but an apostate is somebody who has in fact made a profession of faith, joined the church, and then later repudiated the faith. Many Christians believe that a person who is truly born of the Spirit of God and was truly converted, justified, and in a state of grace can fall away. In other words, some believe that it's possible for a Christian to commit apostasy.

Others in the church believe that once a person is in a state of grace and has been reborn of the Spirit, that person will never fall away. That is sometimes called *eternal security*, or others call it the *perseverance of the saints*. I hold this view myself; I don't believe that a Christian can ever truly and finally fall away. I believe that Christians can sin and can sin radically; they can fall and can fall radically, but they cannot sin and fall fully and finally. I hold the view that if you have it, you never lose it, and if you lose it, you never had it. As John said in 1 John 2:19, "They went out from us, but they were not of us." They were among them. They had made professions of faith. They feigned being Christians, and then they later repudiated the faith.

Let's leave the question of whether a Christian can lose his salvation aside for now. What is being addressed by this text in Hebrews is the impossibility of an apostate's being restored. It's impossible to restore him to repentance if, after he has been enlightened and participated in the Holy Spirit and so on, he commits apostasy. The difficulty of this text, first of all, is with this question: Of what kind of person is the author of Hebrews speaking here? Is he speaking of a Christian who commits apostasy, or is he speaking of someone who made a false profession of faith?

Imagine a drawing on a chalkboard. There's a big circle on the chalkboard, and that circle represents the visible church. Everything outside that visible church represents those who are unchurched, and for the purposes of this discussion, I'm going to refer to those outside this circle as unbelievers. There is, of course, the possibility that there are true believers who for one reason or another are outside the pale of the church, as Augustine said, but for the most part believers exist within the church. Now picture a line in the middle of that circle, bisecting it. On one side of the line are the believers within the church, or what Christ calls the wheat; on the other side of the line are the unbelievers, who are the tares or weeds (see Matt. 13:24–43). Jesus described His church as a mixed body, what Augustine called a *corpus permixtum*. That is, the visible church is always made up of true believers and false professors, people who make a false profession of faith, as Jesus said it was possible to do. Jesus, quoting Isaiah, said this of the Pharisees and scribes: "This people honors me with their lips, but their heart is far from me" (Matt. 15:8). In addition, Paul states that not everybody who was in Israel was of Israel, that not all the Jews in the Old Testament were believers (Rom. 9:6–13). Some were and some were not, even though they were all within the commonwealth of Israel and all within the covenant community.

The question is which of these three groups the author of Hebrews is speaking of when he says that "it is impossible, in the case of those who have once been enlightened, who have tasted the heavenly gift, and have shared in the Holy Spirit, and have tasted the goodness of the word of God and the powers of the age to come, and then have fallen away, to restore them again to repentance" (Heb. 6:4–6). Does he mean unbelievers, true believers, or false professors? First let's note what the author did *not* say. He did not say that it is impossible for a believer, if that believer commits apostasy, to be restored. Nor does he say that it is impossible for those who have been converted to Christ, if they commit apostasy, to be restored again. What he does is to give us a string of clauses to describe this group for whom it is impossible to be restored to repentance.

These people are said to be people who were once "enlightened." They had "tasted the heavenly gift." They had become partakers of the Holy Spirit and "tasted the goodness of the word of God." That certainly sounds as if the author of Hebrews is describing Christians, doesn't it? Who else has been enlightened, tasted of the heavenly gift, become partakers of the Holy Spirit, and tasted the good Word of God and the powers of the age to come? Who else but Christians? There is somebody else of whom these things could be said. Unbelievers in the church sit under the preaching of the gospel and have access to the light of the gospel, and so in a certain sense it could be said of them that they are enlightened by the Word of God, have tasted of His good gifts, and have participated in the sacrament. They taste the bread and the wine. They taste the Word of God with their ears, if you will. They get a taste of the truth. They get a taste of it figuratively and literally in terms of the sacrament and the Word. It doesn't necessarily mean that they're converted.

The description of having "shared in the Holy Spirit" is a little bit more difficult. The church is called the *hagioi*, the "holy ones," who have been consecrated or set apart by the Holy Spirit. The church is the primary focal point of the sanctifying activity of the Holy Ghost. Anybody who is present in the assembly in worship and in the life of the church is participating in some way in the present work of the Holy Spirit. That work may not be penetrating or working in such people, but they are partaking as noninvolved and noncommitted participants. Of course, it could also be said that they've tasted the good Word of God and the powers of the age to come in the same noninvolved and noncommitted participatory way.

When I first started to struggle with this passage many years ago, I concluded that this is what is being described here: the unbelievers who are present within the church are those people who are certainly capable of apostasy and are certainly capable of renouncing Christ whom they once professed. I've since changed my mind.

I've now concluded that the author is describing Christians, which makes this an excruciatingly difficult passage for one who believes that Christians will persevere and will not fall away, that once you have salvation, you can't lose it. If a person doesn't believe in the perseverance of the saints or eternal security, he doesn't have to struggle with this text the way I have to struggle with it, nevertheless I still hold firmly to the idea that a Christian cannot lose his salvation. How can I come to the conclusion that the author of Hebrews is describing Christians? The thing that is pivotal for me is his statement that it is impossible "to restore them again to repentance." To restore somebody again to repentance presupposes that he's previously repented at least once.

Some caution is necessary at this point because the Bible speaks of two different kinds of repentance. There is the repentance of godliness or contrition that is a fruit of the work of the Holy Spirit within a person. The same author also speaks of a repentance of Esau, who, though he repented in tears, did not truly repent and was not restored because his repentance was that which we call the repentance of attrition rather than contrition. Contrition is a repentance motivated by a broken and a contrite heart. Attrition is a repentance that is motivated by a fear of punishment whereby somebody repents in order to get a ticket out of hell. It's like your little child who says she's sorry when she's caught with her hand in the cookie jar. She's sorry that she's going to have to face consequences, but she's not sorry that she has done something wrong. Caution again is necessary, but there's really no reason for me to assume here in this text that the author is speaking about anything else other than authentic repentance, of repentance of contrition. If he is speaking about authentic repentance, then he must be speaking about Christians.

I wish I knew for certain who wrote the book of Hebrews, and I wish I knew for sure to whom it was written. Even more importantly, I wish I knew what issue the author was addressing because there are several possibilities, not the least of which was the threat in the so-called *lapsi* controversy, in which Christians gave their lives as martyrs out of loyalty to Christ. They became human torches in the gardens of Nero, animal meat in the arena, and so on. Not everybody was faithful; there were those who recanted and denied Christ. Not only did they deny Christ, but they also betrayed their fellow Christians. After the heat settled down, the church had to deal with the issue of what to do with these people who had betrayed others who now want to come back into the church. Could they be restored? Maybe that's what the issue was here. The author says, "You have not yet resisted to the point of shedding your blood" (Heb. 12:4).

Another possibility is that the same issue that plagued the Galatians was also an issue here—namely, the Judaizing heresy, which called people back to Old Testament ceremonial Judaism. This was an issue of being bound to carry out all the rituals of the Old Testament as a matter of faith. Paul had put his curse on that heresy in the epistle to the Galatians because it was fundamentally a denial of the finished work of Christ. One of the things that Paul does, and certainly the other Apostles do as well, is to argue in a way whereby he takes the position of his opponent and carries it to its logical conclusion.

Suppose that the author of Hebrews is addressing people who are being persuaded to embrace the Judaizing heresy. I can conceive of the author's warning them to think about this in the following manner: "If after you've been enlightened and tasted the heavenly gift—that is, after you're in Christ—you now want to go back to Judaism and its rituals, if you repudiate the cross and God's salvation, what other salvation is left? There's no possibility of finding salvation by going back." Perhaps that's what we have here in this text.

What gives me the ultimate relief is the author's statement beginning in Hebrews 6:9: "Though we speak in this way, yet in your case, beloved, we feel sure of better things—things that belong to salvation." This causes me to breathe a sigh of relief. I can just hear the author acknowledging that he's speaking in a certain manner, which is not the normal manner; he's saying that he is persuaded of better things about his readers. The author doesn't really think these people are going to do this because he is "sure of better things—things that belong to salvation." In other words, he says: "If you did repudiate Christ, there would be no hope for you, but I'm not worried that you will repudiate Christ or commit apostasy because I'm persuaded that you are Christians and that you will do better things than this."

Though this passage in Hebrews 6 may instill terror in your soul, I commend to you this chapter in its entirety. Take the time this day not just to read this particular passage that is so troublesome but to read the entire chapter because the last part of chapter 6 of Hebrews is one of the most assuring passages that we find anywhere in Scripture. We find the promise of God to keep His promise of covenant and of His faithfulness to His people. If there's any text that gives us comfort and rest in our souls and gives us the confidence that we will not finally become apostate, it's Hebrews 6. Read it carefully, and read it today.

27

Did Jesus Descend into Hell?

1 Peter 3

The hard saying that we will look at in this chapter is one that is deemed hard not because of its harshness but rather because of the great difficulty that attends the understanding of it. It is found in 1 Peter 3, beginning at verse 18. Consider the text, and then allow me to point out the difficulty:

> For Christ also suffered once for sins, the righteous for the unrighteous, that he might bring us to God, being put to death in the flesh but made alive in the spirit, in which he went and proclaimed to the spirits in prison, because they formerly did not obey, when God's patience waited in the days of Noah, while the ark was being prepared, in which a few, that is, eight persons, were brought safely through water. Baptism, which corresponds to this, now saves you, not as a removal of dirt from the body but as an appeal to God for a good conscience, through the resurrection of Jesus Christ, who has gone into heaven and is at the right hand of God, with angels, authorities, and powers having been subjected to him. (vv. 18–22)

The portion of this text that has become a matter of debate and has caused difficulty in reaching agreement has to do with the portion that speaks of Jesus' preaching to the lost spirits in prison. That text then relates to the broader issue of how we understand the statement in the Apostles' Creed that Jesus "was crucified, dead, and buried; he descended into hell; the third day he rose again from the dead." The matter in question is Christ's descent into hell. In ancient theology among the Latin fathers, this was called the *descensus ad inferos*. Some Christians, when reciting the Apostles' Creed, omit the phrase "he descended into hell." In the church where I grew up, we recited that portion of the creed, but in the written form of it in the front of the hymnal there was an asterisk at that phrase, which indicated that there was some question about it.

The Apostles' Creed was so called not because it was produced by the Apostles but because the early church desired to give a summary statement of the teaching of the Apostles. The earliest copy of the creed that we have containing the phrase "descended into hell" is from the middle of the third century, around the year 250. That doesn't mean that it wasn't in the original, but there are questions as to whether it was indeed in the original.

That historical question, however, is not nearly as important as the theological understanding of the significance of this phrase "he descended into hell." The question immediately arises: If Jesus did descend into hell, when did He descend into hell, and why? The most common interpretation is that after Jesus' death on the cross, He made a visit to hell. The time frame is usually considered to be between Christ's death and resurrection.

Then the second question is, If Jesus did descend into hell, why did He do so? Again, different interpretations have been made. Some theologians have taught that the reason that Jesus descended into hell was to complete the full measure of the atonement. Since God's divine judgment on sin involves punishment in hell, if Jesus was going to make a full satisfaction of God's judgment and justice, it would require that He actually go to hell and not merely suffer on the cross outside the gates of Jerusalem. More often, the view of those who say that Jesus went to hell between His death and resurrection is that He went there on a mission of redemption—He went there to free the captives who were being held in hell. Some versions say that the saints of the Old Testament, people such as Abraham and the rest who were believers, were not able to enter heaven until Jesus had actually accomplished His work of redemption in history, so the Old Testament saints were in a kind of waiting area in the meantime. This is where the idea of limbo came from. This doctrine is usually spoken of in association with infants who die in infancy because the Roman Catholic Church teaches that unbaptized infants go to limbo at the time of their death. Though it is considered to be a portion of hell, it is at the extreme outer edges of hell where the flames of divine wrath do not penetrate. This is called the limbo of infants, while the holding place where the believers of the Old Testament had to go to await the finished work of Christ is called the limbo of the fathers or the limbo of the patriarchs.

A host of theological problems are associated with this idea of Christ's descent into hell. The first question we must ask is whether the Bible teaches that Jesus actually descended into hell in any localized place. When you look at the biblical accounts of Jesus' death and resurrection, there's no hint of this idea. We know where Jesus' body was between His death and His resurrection. His body was in the tomb, and we presume to know something about where He was in His soul or in His spirit for two reasons.

On the one hand, at the conclusion of the experience of crucifixion, Jesus spoke aloud to the Father, saying, "Father, into your hands I commit my spirit!" (Luke 23:46). That doesn't mean that the Father necessarily took His spirit at that moment, but the suggestion is, at least, that Jesus finished His work on the cross. That's an important consideration. Jesus does say, "It is finished" (John 19:30), and when He says that, He uses a word borrowed from the economic language of the day that means He made the final payment. Therefore, Reformed theology teaches that Jesus fulfilled all the requirements of redemption and of atonement while He was on the cross. Certainly, if He did descend into hell, He didn't do it to suffer any more, but He went there, if at all, on a redemptive preaching mission to preach to the lost spirits there. The other consideration was Jesus' statement to the thief on the cross, "Today you will be with me in paradise" (Luke 23:43), which seems to suggest that Jesus expected to go that very day from the cross into paradise, and paradise was certainly not to be equated with hell. So if we just look at the Gospels, there would be precious little reason to assume that Jesus went anywhere else but heaven while His human body rested in the tomb.

But then we have the difficult passage in Peter's writings where he says that "he went and proclaimed to the spirits in prison, because they formerly did not obey" (1 Peter 3:19–20). If you go out and get commentaries on 1 Peter, you might find ten different interpretations of this text. It's very difficult to unravel. Let's look specifically at this phrase "he went and proclaimed to the spirits in prison." Notice that Peter doesn't say that Jesus went and preached to dead people in hell. Peter says that "he went and proclaimed to the spirits in prison." Many think that this refers to preaching to the dead because Peter uses the term "spirits." We associate spirits with departed spirits, not with living people. We have to be careful here, because in the Bible, sometimes this word "spirit" is used to refer to people who are still alive. In fact, when God created Adam and Eve, He breathed into them His breath, and we are told that man became a living *nephesh*, a living spirit or a living soul. Sometimes we talk like that in our own language. For example, we might comment on how many people went to the art exhibit last week; if it was a dismal failure, somebody might reply with, "There wasn't a single soul there." We talk like that when we refer to many souls, and we mean many people. So the word itself, "spirit," does not necessarily communicate the idea of dead people.

If you put together "spirits" with "in prison," the New Testament does sometimes speak of hell in metaphorical terms with respect to the concept of a prison. Jesus Himself says: "And you [will] be put in prison. . . . You will never get out until you have paid the last penny" (Matt. 5:25–26), suggesting an analogy between hell and a prison. But again, that's not the only place or the only way that the New Testament uses the concept of imprisonment. We can go back to Jesus' first sermon that He preaches when He comes into the synagogue and reads the text of Isaiah 61:1: "The Spirit of the Lord GOD is upon me, because the LORD has anointed me to bring good news to the poor . . . , to proclaim liberty to the captives." The messianic mission of Jesus was understood by Jesus Himself and the New Testament writers as involving the liberation of people who were being held captive by sin and by Satan. We don't necessarily have to interpret this text to mean that Jesus went to release dead people from hell. It could very easily refer to Jesus' mission of releasing the captives from prison during His earthly life.

Notice again earlier in the text that "Christ also suffered once for sins, the righteous for the unrighteous, that he might bring us to God, being put to death in the flesh but made alive in the spirit, in which he went and proclaimed to the spirits in prison" (1 Peter 3:18–19). The thrust of Peter's statement is that Jesus Christ was raised from the dead by the power of the same Holy Spirit that enabled Him to preach to the spirits in prison. It doesn't say anything about when He was preaching to the spirits in prison, only that He was doing this mission under the same power of the Holy Spirit by which He was resurrected. It's very possible that all that this text is saying is that Jesus Christ was raised by the power of the Holy Spirit, which is the same Spirit that anointed Him to His earthly mission of liberating the prisoners who were the children of Abraham, the Jewish people. This is one possible understanding of this text.

Though we struggle with the difficulty of understanding Peter's teaching about Jesus' preaching to the lost spirits in prison, we need to hold on to a couple of things tenaciously. The first is that no matter how we interpret this text, it's clear to us from the Scriptures that everything that was required of Christ to effect our redemption was, in fact, performed. Second, whether Peter was referring to the people who were held captive and were walking around Israel during Jesus' earthly ministry, people who were in limbo, or people in this present age, we know that all of us, apart from that work of Christ, are indeed lost souls and lost spirits. We are in this kind of imprisonment, and the only One who has the power within Himself to release people from that kind of captivity is Christ, and He does that through the same power, the power of the Holy Spirit, by which His body in the tomb was raised from the dead. So He, with the Holy Spirit, raises us from the dead and delivers us from captivity.

About the Author

Dr. R.C. Sproul was founder of Ligonier Ministries, first minister of preaching and teaching at Saint Andrew's Chapel in Sanford, Fla., first president of Reformation Bible College, and executive editor of *Tabletalk* magazine. His radio program, *Renewing Your Mind*, is still broadcast daily on hundreds of radio stations around the world and can also be heard online. He was author of more than one hundred books, including *The Holiness of God*, *Chosen by God*, and *Everyone's a Theologian*. He was recognized throughout the world for his articulate defense of the inerrancy of Scripture and the need for God's people to stand with conviction upon His Word.

HARD
SAYINGS

UNDERSTANDING DIFFICULT
PASSAGES OF SCRIPTURE

R.C. SPROUL

Download the eBook for Free

Go to Ligonier.org/hardsayings
to download the ebook for free.

Your unique code is

0C67-2DFC-B302-CD47

"If there is a shortcut to accelerating your understanding of Scripture, it is to focus your attention on the hard sayings."

—R.C. SPROUL

God gave us His Word so that we may know Him and live by His truth. So what should we do when we're reading the Bible and a difficult passage stops us in our tracks? Sometimes the solution is right there on the page—if we know where to look—while other passages gain clarity in light of the rest of the Bible or its historical background. With the help of an experienced guide, we can overcome the obstacles to our progress and know God's Word more deeply.

In *Hard Sayings*, Dr. R.C. Sproul applies his wisdom as a theologian and Bible teacher to some of the most challenging verses in Scripture. By showing us how to navigate tough texts in the Old and New Testaments, he outlines key principles to help us grow in our knowledge of God.

LIGONIER MINISTRIES

ISBN 978-1-64289-461-5

9 781642 894615

RELIGION / Biblical Studies / General